COLLEGE

The Best Five Years of Your Life

Clark Benson and Alex Gordon

PUBLICATIONS

Bridgeport, Connecticut

To our parents. Without their love, guidance and money, we never would have made it through college.

Disclaimer

Some of the material in this book may, if you were to follow our advice, get you arrested, expelled, or otherwise in really big trouble (or at least embarrassed). We assume basic intelligence in our reader and know that it won't be you running around with a lampshade on your head.

ISBN 1-887166-13-0

Cover and text design by David Charlsen & Others

Photographs used with permission from Underwood Photo Archives, San Francisco

Printed in the United States

For more information, contact:

HYSTERIA
PUBLICATIONS

Post Office Box 8581
Bridgeport, CT 06605
Tel.: 203.333.9399
Fax.: 203.367.7188
Web: http://www.hysteriabooks.com
Email: laugh@hysteriabooks.com

Distributed to the trade by Andrews and McMeel
Order department and customer service toll-free number:
800.826.4216

Orders only fax: 800.437.8683

Contents

Acknowledgments

The authors would like to thank the following people: Deborah Werksman, Lysbeth Guillorn, Julie Kaufmann-Gordon, Gregory Kallenberg, Suzy Cekal, Craig Aaron, the DeMars sisters, Peter Orner, Lori Scalise, Joel and Sue, the interns at INsider, The Shalamar, the residents of 1328 Forest Ct. and 1102 S. Forest, T & B Palace #2, and our friends and colleagues who have been kind enough to lend their support, wisdom and kindness to this project.

Introduction

Contrary to what cynics may say, America's universities don't just create cardboard-cutout corporate worker bees. Neither do they only churn out information-overload slacker couch potatoes. That's not to say that colleges don't produce both of these types in legions, because they do. It's just that people who come away from college with nothing more than a fancy piece of paper and/or vague knowledge of a field in which they'll probably never work have nobody to blame but themselves.

This book is not so much about college as it is about the college *lifestyle*. It's easy to go through college and never really *experience* the incredibly open-ended possibilities of it. For example, everyone knows students who go home every weekend to Mom and Dad's suburban security blanket or to their high school boyfriend/girlfriend. These types might as well just send for a diploma off the back of a matchbook cover.

College is a privilege meant to be abused, and immersing yourself fully in your books is *not* the way to get the most of it. In the "real world" it helps to have social skills too, you know.

"The friends you make in college will stay with you for the rest of your life," is as cliché-ridden as it gets, but no truer statement has ever been told. At what other time in your life, for example, can you watch *Caddyshack, Fletch, Wayne's World,* and the like every night, quote lines from them *ad nauseam*, and find a bunch of friends to do it with? When else (barring some serious prison time) are you literally *forced* to get to know a diverse bunch of people simply because you live, eat, sleep, and shower every day in close proximity to them? You'll know you've gotten used to college on the day the realization hits you that you and your friends use exactly the same slang, not to mention hand gestures and other more subtle quirks.

Not only is college a terrific playground for finding and hanging out with a bunch of close friends, but truly, unless you become a rock star or tabloid celebrity, you will never have access to such vast numbers of the opposite sex. If after four years of college you find it impossible to get a date, it may be time to seriously consider throwing in the towel and joining a monastery or convent after graduation.

College is also about the only chance you'll have to be a complete tightwad and still find it socially acceptable, even kind of hip. College students live *cheaply*. And sure, once you get into the swing of college your lifestyle may seem incredibly hectic, but when else will you have such opportunities for volunteer work, supporting causes, and doing other worthwhile things, not to mention good old-fashioned, American-style partying.

Enough of this wishy-washy stuff. After all, this isn't one of those lame hippy-dippy "self-help" guides.

CHAPTER 1

CHOOSING A COLLEGE

Deciding where to go to college is an arduous process. High school seniors spend long, sleepless nights agonizing over it, and even the ones with good enough grades to get in anywhere they choose spend endless hours applying to and visiting many different schools. Parents cajole and badger their kids, dragging them across the country to make sure they go to *the right school.* Is it really worth it? All said and done, college is college, and much of the anguish can be avoided by answering a few simple questions.

1) Do I want a big or small school?
Here are a few subtle differences you might want to consider:

The Big School vs. the Small School

Big School	Small School
• Boasts many famous alumni	• "Isn't that where Dan Quayle went?"
• People have stereotypical view of your school	• People say "No, what *college* did you go to?"
• You tell everyone your sexual escapades	• Everyone tells you they heard about your sexual escapades
• Big-time NCAA football and basketball	• You start on football and basketball teams
• World-renowned professors do earthbreaking research in your backyard	• Not-so-famous professors actually teach your classes
• Local radio station broadcasts alternative rock, college sports, and politically radical talk shows	• Local radio station broadcasts crop reports, pork futures, and barometer readings
• Tough to find parking around campus	• Tough to find campus to park around
• School name: _____ State	• School name: St. _____
• School has study-abroad programs in London, Paris, and Florence	• School has study "abroad" program in Canada
• Book needed for term paper has been checked out of university library	• Library never owned book needed for term paper
• School president worries about ethnic diversity, racial quotas, and state funding	• School president worries about your health, whether you're eating right, and how you did on your Bio test
• Smashing Pumpkins sells out your school's basketball arena	• Survivor and Loverboy headline the county fair
• Lots of college bars, one cool one	• One college bar
• Sip cappuccino and discuss Sartre into the wee hours at local coffeehouse	• Rush to Sam's Market for instant Taster's Choice packets before it closes at 7 p.m.

2) How expensive a college can I (in other words, my parents) afford?

Obviously, don't go somewhere so costly that your parents will have to resort to embezzlement or fraud to pay your tuition. While elsewhere in this book we advise milking parents for all they're worth, we don't mean this literally. You can always take out student loans, but you may be living on ramen noodles until you're forty-something.

3) How far away is the school?

Two to five hours away is the ideal distance for a "close to home" school, usually one of your state's universities. Anything closer and you'll be too tempted to cop-out and go home every weekend. Plus, if your school is too close to home the specter of your parents dropping in unexpectedly on Sunday mornings will always be on your mind. A school over five hours away but not far enough away to fly means hellishly long drives or bus rides.

"Away" schools (those which are farther than a few states from home) have different location criteria. Since you are too far away to make it back for weekends, find out how far away the campus is from beaches, ski hills, major cities, Civil War battle sites, and other points of interest. Also be sure you can at least get home for Thanksgiving. Nothing is more depressing than being alone on a college campus during Thanksgiving weekend, (except perhaps being alone on campus during Spring Break).

4) Does this school have a good program in my area of study?

Oh, give it a rest. Almost everybody changes majors three or four times, and many students don't even bother choosing one before their junior year, when most schools insist upon it. Obviously if you've planned on becoming an engineer since you got your first Erector Set you want a school with a good engineering program, but the rest of us wishy-washy slobs plan on waiting until the *last* minute to make the wrong decision.

5) Am I going to like the people at this school?
I don't know, *are* you?

6) How long is the application? Are there essays?
This is without a doubt the single most important aspect of choosing a college. Do you really want to spend 10 to 20 hours filling out a complicated application and writing sappy essays for a school that's probably going to reject you anyhow? If you're applying to 10 different schools? It's up to you, of course, but they say your senior year in high school is one of the best times of your life. Are you going to sit inside wracking your brain to fill out paperwork while your going-nowhere high school pals are out having a blast? Of course not. Find a few choice schools that you have a realistic chance of getting into, or take the easy way out—apply to state schools that process 30,000 applications a year and by necessity have one- or two-page admission forms.

Big State School Application

INSTRUCTIONS:
FILL OUT, ADD POSTAGE, AND MAIL

PLACE
STAMP
HERE

First Initial, Last Name: _____

Zip Code: _____

GPA: _____ SAT: _____

Essay (optional): Why are you any
different than the other 20,000
students applying here? (be realistic
and please limit to 20 words)

State Tech University
Admissions Office
14 State Street
Campustown, Big State
12345-1234

_____
_____
_____

Small Private School Application

St. Vinnie of Argyle Academy
and Teachers College

Name: _____ Address: _____

Date of birth: __ / __ / __   Nickname: _____

City: _____ State: ____ Zip code (Plus 4): _____-_____

Phone: (day) ___-___-____ (night) ___-___-____ Fax: ___-___-____

Pager: ___-___-____ Email: _____

URL: _____ Birthmarks: _____

Who to reach in case of emergency? _____

And what if they're not in? _____

Astrological sign: _____

Average daily cholesterol intake: _____

Shoe size: _____ Height: _____ Weight: _____

Hair: _____ Eyes: _____ Ears: _____

GPA: _____ SAT: _____ SS#: ___-__-____

ACT: _____ IQ: _____ RBIs: _____

MCI bill: $_____ $x + 2xy - y^2 =$ _____

Class rank: _____ Tetris high score: _____

I'm thinking of a number between 1 and 10. What is it? ___

Close, guess a little higher ___

Last movie seen: _____

How many stars would you give it? _____

Are you bringing any fruit or vegetables into the college?

_____

Essays:
1) Describe an especially traumatic experience in your life and how you overcame it. _____
_____

Did this experience more resemble a made-for-TV movie, a docudrama, or a full-blown Hollywood blockbuster? _____
_____

2) If you could invite anyone to dinner who would it be and why? Would you serve pasta? _____
_____

3) If you were a fish what kind of a tree would you be? _____
_____

4) ¿Quien es mas macho? ¿Ricardo Montalban o Lloyd Bridges?
_____

Explica: _____
_____
_____

5) If it was only a "three-hour tour" how come Mr. and Mrs. Howell had so many changes of clothes? _____
_____

6) What do you see here?_____
_____
_____
_____
_____

7) Describe in detail the feelings you had during birth and how the experience of being born will help make you an involved and integral member of our student body. _____
_____

8) Why, just why? _____
_____
_____
_____

CHAPTER 2

STARTING SCHOOL

Summer Orientation

Most schools have summer orientation programs for incoming students, which have the effect of making college seem much more intimidating than it really is. If you know a few things about orientation before going in, you will be able to breathe much easier:

- Those student orientation leaders are *paid* to be so overzealous about their school.

- Your "campus tour" will reflect the biases of your tour guide. (Don't worry, the theater building isn't really everyone's favorite campus hangout.)

- Be leery of making friends in your orientation group. For the next four years, you may be stuck with some complete dork surprising you at parties, giving you a big hug and blubbering, "This was my first friend at school!"

- Make a funny face when posing for your school ID[1] picture. This will make for a great conversation piece in the years to come.

- Buy a couple of pieces of school clothing when you attend orientation. Wash and wear them over the rest of the summer, and when you return in the fall you will look like a campus veteran.

- Caution: if you have to pick your first semester's classes at orientation, don't take it lightly, or a semester of Assyrian literature, advanced Keynesian macroeconomics, and fourth-year Russian may be yours.

- Ignore all of what you are being told, as you will forget it by the fall anyway.

. . . And most importantly,

- School is much better than orientation will lead you to believe.

---

[1] **School ID** (*n*) - a card that is essential to your daily existence, not only for charging books and getting into university events, but because it is usually the easiest form of identification to doctor for illicit purposes. It can be taken for granted that you will lose your student ID at least three or four times during your college career, usually at inopportune moments like class registration.

Packing

If you are being driven to school it is essential to cram as much stuff as humanly possible into the family sport utility vehicle. Forget about traveling light, the more junk you can bring down to school, the more creature comforts you will have with you, and the less money you will have to spend down the line. Gut your car so no potential storage space is overlooked; empty the glove compartment, leave the spare tire at home, even remove a seat or two if you must. Use the car's roof to transport carpet remnants, wading pools, or any other furnishing necessities.

Packing your car may come down to do or die, especially if you have a large wardrobe or a love of hi-tech products. If you simply have to leave some stuff home, you can survive without some of the following items:

Extra set of speakers. You can live without "surround sound" for a semester, and besides, your roommate will probably bring a set.

Hot air popcorn popper. Your parents are sure to make you bring one of these. Apparently when mom and dad were in school their entire social life consisted of having people over and making popcorn. Along with the popper, they'll send you off with a five-pound bag of popping corn, which will inevitably explode all over your dorm room the first time you try to open it. Of course, finding popcorn kernels in every nook and cranny provides an amusing hobby for the rest of the semester. Mom and dad haven't yet caught on that *nobody* bothers to pop their own corn anymore, unless perhaps they're nuking a packet of lite microwave cheese popcorn.

High school yearbooks. They take up space on the bookshelf and make you look like you're living off memories. Besides, you don't really want your new friends to find out that you were the point man of the Chess Team, do you?

Typewriter. Hel-lo! Haven't you heard? We are now in the Information Age.

Even if your typewriter is one of those word processing ones with a memory, we still wouldn't recommend bringing it to school with you. Do the smart thing. Go down to the lab and learn how to use a computer.

Prom dress. While you may go to a couple of formal events your first year, people will recognize a prom dress when they see one. Not only will you be snickered at, you will also most likely be carded.

Stuffed animals. If you must, bring a few of the most sentimental ones and leave the rest at home. Be sure to include the one your high school sweetheart gave you, though—it comes in handy as an outlet for your frustrations after you are dumped.

Mom. One parent driving you to school is enough, and if packing comes down to the space that mom takes up in the car or your neon signs, which do you think is more important? Hell, she's gonna cry anyway.

The First Week

Your first week of college is crucial. Depending on how fragile your emotions are, the first week may set the course for your whole year. While the start of college may be a blast, it can also be tough. Amuse yourself by exploring your surroundings, and don't let a lame first week turn you into a morose and bitter drop-out or a terminal dorm-room hermit.

CDs You Will Never Need to Own

The following compact discs are integral parts of even the lamest collegiate CD collections. Your roommate, neighbor, or at the very least someone down the hall will own them, so why not just borrow? $15 a disc is a hell of a lot for the average college student to shell out; in fact, if you don't already have one, you may find it to your advantage to bring just a CD *player* without any actual *discs*, as college is the Land of Plenty when it comes to borrowing other people's music.

- *The Steve Miller Band's Greatest Hits*
- Nirvana: *Nevermind*
- *Legend: The Best of Bob Marley*
- Jimmy Buffett: *Songs You Know and Love*
- The Cure: *Standing on a Beach: The Singles*
- James Taylor: *Greatest Hits*
- Alanis Morrissette: *Jagged Little Pill*
- Pink Floyd: *The Wall*
- Anything by Metallica, U2, R.E.M., or Van Halen (David Lee Roth–era only)
- Pearl Jam: *Ten*
- *The Best of The Doors*
- Dave Matthews Band: *Under the Table and Dreaming*
- Grateful Dead: *Skeletons from the Closet*
- Tori Amos: *Under the Pink*
- Blues Traveler: *Four*

New Roommates

It may sound trite, but don't judge your roommates by first impressions. Just because your new roomie wants to hang a velvet Billy Ray Cyrus or Luke Perry tapestry on the wall doesn't mean he's a complete goon—there may be sarcasm involved. And that friendly, outgoing roomie whom you like immediately may be covering up more emotional problems than the entire cast of *Diff'rent Strokes.*

If nothing else, a "bizarre" roommate is, to use the old cliché, a "character builder." In other words, you will take on the task of building your roomie's character. Look at this as a challenge; "How can I make this person socially acceptable?" A weirdo roommate *is* a fantastic conversation piece. For the rest of your college career, you can hold court with tales of the all-night seances your roommate held to communicate with the spirit of Timothy Leary or the necklace of garlic she wore to protect herself from vampires.

Making Friends

Make as many friends as you can right away, as it is always easier to jettison them later than to force your way into existing social groups. If this sounds snobby, it is. But then again, so is Darwinism, capitalism, the NCAA Tourney, and the American way. If you want to sit in the dorm every Saturday night watching basic cable channels in the lounge, go ahead, but don't say we didn't warn you.

Class Registration

If for some reason your schedule is messed up and you have to attend on-campus registration as a first semester freshman, don't even try to figure out what's going on. Find the chaos-ridden registration area, immediately grab

On-campus registration is a relaxing, stress-free chance to ease into the semester.

a group of administrative-type figures and break down completely, begging on your hands and knees for assistance. Someone is certain to take pity on you, the poor clueless freshman in this frenzied den of greed and despair, and guide you hand-in-hand through the necessary registration steps. Trying to handle class registration without help can reduce even the cockiest freshman to a quivering mass of Jell-O.

Buying Books

The selling and repurchasing of textbooks to and from college students is a legalized form of extortion that would turn Don Corleone green with envy. Every semester, students pay top dollar prices for books they may never crack open. And after everyone has been fleeced for a couple hundred bucks at the beginning of the semester, the typical professor will decide the material in the textbooks isn't all that great, and will assign additional "readings" or "note packets" that have to be purchased from a copy shop.

After shelling out all this cash, you would figure you could recoup at least half of your money by selling your books back after finals. Big wrong. Regardless of the condition a book is in, expect no more than $3 for a typical $48 textbook. The bookstore clerk will always tell you that your book is not on order for the next semester, and will pretend to be doing you a favor by taking the heavy volume off your hands. "I might be able to ship it to our distributor, who may be able to find a small teacher's college in North Dakota that can use it. . ." the clerk will say of your hardly used, $63 Advanced Nuclear Physics text.

At this point you will most likely get possessive about the book. "Two dollars? Two measly dollars? Forget it, I'll keep it," you will decide in disgust, thinking in an irrational rage that *The A-to-Z Guide to Far Eastern Horticulture* will be a fine addition to your personal library and a valuable reference tool in the future. Of course, this unwieldy volume will end up in a dumpster as soon as you realize the book isn't even worth the trouble of lugging home.

Though the university and the bookstores are certainly not blameless, the professors who assign the books are the subtle fiends behind this ritual gouging. Many professors write textbooks themselves, and if they assign you someone else's book, the odds are pretty good that the writer is a friend of theirs. Textbooks "change" every year—a Newly Revised Fifth Edition is almost exactly the same as last year's Newly Revised Fourth Edition, with perhaps a different cover and new introduction (as if anyone ever reads the introduction to a textbook). "New Edition" means new royalties to the writer, and the process of higher learning goes on.

In recent years, some enterprising students have organized textbook collectives where you can "borrow" books and "donate" books along the socialist model. Of course, these collectives usually operate with the efficiency of their former Eastern European counterparts.

One final note—be wary of buying used books. Sometimes a student will "sabotage" books before selling them back. Somehow the sting of losing 95 percent of your textbook investment is greatly reduced if you've ripped out entire chapters of the books you're selling back.

School Supplies

Notebooks/Folders. Yeah, it's really school-spirited to buy the ones with the university emblem on them, but are they worth the extra two dollars? The only real difference is that you will be doodling on "University of _____" instead of "Mead" when your thoughts wander during a lecture. Also be sure to avoid glossy-covered notebooks or folders, as all the phone numbers and little notes you write on them will rub off on your hands.

Pens/Pencils. Buy pens at the beginning of the semester even though you are certain to lose them within a few weeks. Everyone on campus must contribute to the supply of lost pens so that there will be ones to find later when you look behind the cushions of couches, on library shelves, or in your back pocket. Pencils are too commonplace to actually purchase, but before you go stealing them from just anywhere it may be smart to ask your golf pro or bowling alley attendant if those short, stubby ones are #2's.

Backpacks/Book bags. Each school has different unwritten laws on how students should carry their books. A backpack is the universal norm, but the one-shoulder vs. two-shoulder debate rages on. Of course, two-shoulder is the ergonomically correct way to carry a pack and the only practical way if you are riding a bike or in-line skating to class. Still, there are those student bodies that insist on the one-shoulder method despite the fact that the pack always slips off, feels awkward and can lead to chiropractic problems.

Blue books. Most colleges require you to purchase these books for essay exams. Blue books consist of a flimsy blue cover wrapped around some notebook paper. Why you can't just use your own notebook paper instead of having to run to the bookstore three minutes before your exam to shell out 17 cents for one of these is up there with the Loch Ness Monster as one of life's great unsolved mysteries.

CHAPTER 3

ROOM AND BOARD

College life begins in the dorms. Any misgivings you have about college are sure to be fully realized the moment you arrive at your dormitory. The term "dorm room" carries with it the image of a small, stark, cold room with flimsy mattresses and a single 40-watt light bulb hanging from the ceiling. In other words a prison cell without the bars. And of course, you will have to share this cell with one or more complete strangers.

Your dormitory itself isn't the Ritz-Carlton, to say the least. Dormitories tend come from two schools of architecture: pre-World War II, musty brick structures that are starting to show their age (but they have such *character!*), or 1950s–60s tacky, institutional, function-over-form cubes.

You will need some time to adjust to the dorm lifestyle. Always eating dinner between the hours of 4:30 and 6:30, hearing your neighbor's stereo cranking the same bad tunes over and over, and sharing a communal bathroom may take a little getting used to. But once you have adjusted to the change, you'll find that dorm life has a likable charm of its own—for about two weeks.

Dorm Furnishings

Milk Crates

Milk crates are de rigeur in all dorm room decor. In other words, you've got to have some. If you're lucky, a student moving out will pass some on to you. Otherwise, you'll be reduced to begging at the local convenience store or, god forbid, actually shelling out some cash at Kmart.

Carpeting

Carpeting is necessary to soak up all the beer and assorted liquids you will spill on your floor and to give visiting out-of-town friends some small degree of comfort when they pass out with nowhere else to sleep. Don't rush out to buy it, though, as some entrepreneur will usually appear outside your dorm early in the semester with a U-Haul full of cheap carpet remnants in colors ranging from puce to institutional gray.

Futon

These New Age wonders are the biggest scam going. Supposedly the ultimate in comfort, but can you really fit one in your dorm room? If you are determined to spend the money, try the comfort of a Craft-Matic adjustable bed.

TV, VCR

These appliances can rescue a boring collegiate existence or just as easily wreck a promising academic one. If you need your daily dose of reruns, you obviously want a television, whether your grades suffer or not. A VCR, however, may not be the best idea, as it means the riff-raff from your dorm floor will be constantly hanging out and watching dumb movies in your room. Why not just intrude on the privacy of a friend with a VCR down the hall and save the expense? On the other hand, though, the ability to catch a flick in the privacy of your own room can be a way to attract members of the opposite sex.

Stereo

That clock radio or boom box you've had since 7th grade may do the trick, but your room will never turn into a true "hangout" unless it has a decent stereo. The ability to blast loud tunes at any time of the day or night is essential to establishing your place in the dorm stereo wars. A CD player with repeat allows you to torment your hallmates to no end—find a copy of *The Carpenters' Greatest Hits*, hit repeat on track 2 ("Top of the World"), turn the volume up to "11," and leave for the day, locking your door behind you.

Beer Signs

The initial degree of respect a freshman guy gets on his dorm floor is determined by the beer signs he has hanging on his walls. Authentic neon ones are cooler than plastic, Moosehead signs beat Miller's Genuine Draft signs, a sign in the shape of your state or a football helmet blows away a plain brewing company logo, and so forth in the hierarchy of beer sign coolness.

Government Property

Stolen road signs and the like, though perhaps not as essential as they were in the '70s, are still used for atmosphere in the dorm rooms of freshman males. A big "BRIDGE FREEZES BEFORE ROAD" sign laid horizontally on a milk crate makes an instant coffee table. Lots of government property is there for the taking on college campuses, since parts of every campus always seem to be under construction. While construction horses may take up too much space in a cramped dorm room, those annoying yellow lights that never stop blinking are great window decorations.

One caveat—stealing government property is illegal. There's nothing quite as embarrassing as getting kicked out of school for a semester for taking a "NO PARKING" sign.

Posters, Wall Hangings, etc.

You've obviously got to cover up those sickly yellow dorm room walls with something. Posters and prints work best, although neo-hippies will invariably fill half the room with a parachute-sized tie-dye tapestry. Be creative in your choice of wall decorations. Freshmen tend to draw from a pool of about 10 popular posters; stay away from these obvious choices:

Guys' Walls	*Girls' Walls*
Cars, chicks, and chicks with cars	The Solo Flex Guy
Dali's *The Persistence of Memory*	"Hang in There" photo with kitty on ledge
Free beer company T&A posters	Monet's *Waterlilies*
"Body by Budweiser"	Pictures of James Dean, Marilyn Monroe, Jim Morrison or other dead people
Beastie Boys or Phish posters (don't you guys like any other bands?)	That poster with all the babies on it

Refrigerator

Where else are you going to put those promotional magnets with the local pizza place's phone number? Fridges are also places to keep cold soft drinks, beer, and baking soda. They are doubly valuable to the biology or horticulture major, who can study firsthand the fungus, mold and other growths that eventually line the fridge's insides. Companies on campus rent out fridges by the semester at ridiculous rates, which makes fridge ownership an extremely desirable quality in a roommate.

Fan

A fan is crucial, perhaps even more necessary than a bed. There is no greater hell than sitting in 95 degree heat in a stuffy dorm room with a two-week-old pile-up of laundry.

Answering Machine

An answering machine is a necessity if you want any kind of reliable social life, and recording witty answering machine messages can be a fun way to waste time. Just change the more annoying ones after a week or so, and as your parents should be calling every so often, keep the innuendo to a minimum. Do us a favor—since you will forget to give your roommates their messages, please just leave them on the machine.

Computer

A computer is nice to have when you want to get some work done. Since many dorms have in-room dedicated access to the Internet, a computer is also the ultimate time waster of the Information Age. Many a GPA has been ruined by the Net.

Clock Radio

A clock radio is necessary so that you can wake up for about 30 seconds, drowsily rationalize staying in bed, and lose the willpower battle with yourself before going back to bed and blowing off your early classes. Make sure the snooze button is easy to reach and will hold up to repeated bashings.

Message Board

In the first week of school, dorm residents put those write-on rub-off marker boards on their doors so their friends can leave notes. In the second week of school, everyone's board has been vandalized with drunken obscenities scribbled in permanent marker.

Dorm Food

Dorm food has been the butt of more bad jokes than the mother-in-law, so we'll skip the stereotypical gags, such as, "You'd better stop that hamburger; I think it's moving," and "It's Tuesday. Must be mystery meat night." With a little effort you can find an edible meal in any cafeteria.

If you don't like what's on the daily menu, never fear; contemporary dorm cuisine offers alternatives such as huge salad bars, frozen yogurt, and bagels. There is always enough raw material outside of the daily specials to whip something up; just be creative and pray that the microwave is not on the blink. Concocting smorgasbords of different, often disgustingly incompatible foods is a great way to relieve dormitory stir-craziness and exercise your right brain at the same time. A few of our original recipes are included below, and for dessert, the health-unconscious may opt to stir Fruit Loops and Crunch Berries in with soft-serve ice cream or frozen yogurt.

DORM FOOD RECIPES
Clip and save!

Dorm Cafeteria Rice Krispies Squares

Ingredients

> 4 Marshmallows (usually found near
> hot cocoa dispenser)
> Rice Krispies
> Butter or margarine (optional)

Directions

> In bowl, combine ingredients.
> Nuke for a while. Serves ½.

Dorm Cafeteria Garlic Bread

Ingredients

> Hot dogs or hamburgers (as many
> as they let you have)
> Butter or margarine
> Garlic spread (you may have to
> bring this in yourself)

Directions

> Take hot dogs or hamburgers out of
> buns, throw them out. Apply butter
> and garlic spread to buns. Toast or
> microwave until done. Serves 1,
> if lucky.

Dorm Cafeteria Cottage Cheese Collage

Ingredients

> Cottage cheese (a big mound or bowl)
> Anything else on salad bar that looks good

Directions

> Whee! Look at all that cottage cheese!
> What can we put in it? Peas, alfalfa sprouts,
> chow mein noodles, peaches, tofu, French
> dressing, green olives, gherkins, etc. Stir
> and eat. Serves you right.

Dorm Pranks

Living in a dormitory is an opportunity to do all the stupid things you've wanted to do since you were a kid. The depths of goonery exhibited by dorm inhabitants know no boundaries. Dorm pranks are absolutely necessary, as they add a little spark to the day-to-day routine of dormitory life. If targeted correctly, pranks also serve to keep annoying or overzealous dormmates in line. Always remember that the key to a good dorm prank is creativity. Here are some tried-and-true classics, which will hopefully serve to spark your own unique efforts.

Without a doubt, bathrooms are the best locales for dorm pranks, especially since nobody cleans them on weekends. On the dorm floor of one of the authors, two separate large-scale bathroom exhibitions took place in a single semester. On one hot summer day, all drains to the large shower area were stopped up and half the bathroom was completely flooded, filled with suds and turned into a pool/bubble bath. A great time, even though no girls showed up.

The second prank also involved the use of large quantities of water—solidified water. This was in the middle of the winter, and when a big snowstorm hit it was decided to celebrate by building a snowman—*in the middle of the bathroom.* Alas, the anatomically correct snowman, imaginatively named "Frosty," only lasted about two days.

A good "no-brainer" prank is to throw a bucket of water over the stall on someone when they are sitting on the toilet. It's simple, guaranteed to generate a scream, and the only way to get caught is if the person sitting on the pot recognizes the shoes of whoever does the soaking. Along similar lines, a sheet of clear cellophane can be placed *under* the seat of a toilet, causing an obvious complication for the next user.

Another prank that still has its merits is the good old "shaving-cream-in-manilla-envelope-slide-the-open-end-under-door-and-stomp-on-the-envelope" trick, which sprays a closed room with shaving cream. Knock first so the occupant is approaching the door when "creamed."

Cruel pranks like these, though fun, are unoriginal and should only be used for purposes of vengeance. A true prank should be either somehow enlightening or completely baffling to the prankee. For example, comb old *People* magazines or *TV Guide*s for pictures of uncool celebrities. Cut out and stick the photos inside virtually everything the prankee owns, from textbooks to rolled-up socks, cassette tapes, deodorant, medicines, underwear, even the thongs he or she wears to the shower. For months to come this person will be baffled and embarrassed as he or she comes across pictures of Tori Spelling at every turn. Or say you have a really uptight roommate. You can easily use this prank to enlighten him or her—just substitute Zen koans for the celebrity photos.

The RA

RAs, or Resident Advisors, are juniors or seniors who live on a dorm floor as pseudo–chaperones, and have their room and board (and sometimes tuition) paid for by the university. There are three types of RAs.

First, there is the kindergarten-teacher type. This RA will spend hours making construction-paper football and teddy bear name plates for the doors on the floor. Of course, within a few hours on "move-in day," the footballs will have been switched around and the teddy bears will have ended up in obscene positions. But this type of RA doesn't get the hint. Though he or she will initially try to come across as a sort of all-knowing big brother or sister, you will eventually realize that this person is lonelier and has more problems than you and all of your friends combined.

The second type of RA is the stern authoritarian, who has an immaculate room and believes in "discipline, discipline, discipline." Needless to say, he or she has absolutely no sense of humor and loves to "write you up" for infractions like playing indoor ultimate Frisbee, making noise after quiet hours, or pressing all the buttons on the elevator. This type of RA can actually be better than the first type, because an antagonistic RA helps you meet people by giving you something to complain about with everyone else on your floor.

The third and best kind of RA just doesn't give a shit. See no evil, hear no evil, just as long as they don't get in trouble with their higher-ups. Since this type obviously has better things to do with their time than take frustrations out on or buddy up with a bunch of freshmen, they are usually pretty cool people, and ironically the only RAs worth getting to know.

Lofts

If your residence hall allows it, one way to improve your bland room is to build a loft. A loft is a wooden structure that houses your mattress and frees up space by letting you sleep a foot away from the ceiling. A loft can only be properly built by a "handyman" father who comes in for the weekend, swears a lot, and gets sawdust all over everything. Lofts are great ways to make the most out of your limited living space, but they do have their disadvantages. Forget any notions or fantasies of acrobatic sex—attempting to climb into bed with less than your full faculties can result in a dangerous free-fall.

Beyond the Dorms

Dorm life has its advantages (although it's tough to think of any offhand), but most students (i.e., any with a social clue) find that one or two years is all they can take of "university housing". Unless you move into a fraternity or sorority (see Chapter 18) you will live in an apartment, a house, or perhaps a co-op.

A co-op is a sort of independent living arrangement between people who don't know each other. Generally you will have to share a kitchen, bathroom, and political stance with the other members of your co-op. If this isn't enough incentive to stay away, consider this: part of the reason the rent is so low is because you will be expected to do daily cleaning duties. Avoid.

Apartment Living

Moving into an apartment is the college student's first attempt at true independence. While this seems really grown-up and exciting, beware: apartment living brings on actual *responsibility*, or in other words, headaches.

Landlords

There are two types of campus landlords: big, impersonal rental companies and meddling, busybody "mom and pop" types. While you might think you'd prefer the "mom and pop" type, think again—it's kind of like living with parents all over again ("Take the garbage out!" "Are those long-haired freaks friends of yours? They look like fugitives," "Just what exactly do you plan on doing with that keg?").

These types of landlords will start out trying to be your buddy, but watch out if you cross them, such as spilling soda on the carpet or putting a (gasp!) nail in the wall. Then comes the speech: "How could you do this to

Your first apartment.

me, after all I've done for you. Why I've given you three new garbage cans this semester alone! I'm so disappointed." Or the endless guilt trip you'll endure when you try to get them to fix something; " I have a thousand other repairs to do, plus paint my own house, and spend time with my kids, but I suppose you want me to drop everything and come fix your overflowing toilet?"

The other side of the coin is the landlord who owns a big rental company. You have about as much chance of breaking through the bureaucracy and actually getting to see these landlords as you would have getting an audience with the Pope. The one advantage to this type of landlord is that your relationship is so impersonal that when something goes wrong all you have to do is pick up the phone and threaten to sue. Doing this will bring on no guilt as you have never even seen your landlord. You will be pleasantly surprised at how quickly things get done when you invoke the legal system.

Bills

House or apartment living means separate bills for things like heat, telephone, electricity, water, and, most importantly, cable TV. There is only one rule to follow regarding bills; *never* volunteer to put one in your name, as this renders you fully responsible for paying it. Bickering over bills is a major pain. You will find yourself arguing that your roommate should have to pay more of the electric bill since she left her curling iron plugged in over spring break, and spending your free time trying to discover who made the 45-minute call at $2.99 per minute to a psychic hotline.

No matter how friendly you may be with your living mates, they will turn into different creatures when it comes to money. And when the gas bill goes unpaid for five months, the gas company won't care that your roommates have no money. Not only will all your free time be spent dodging bill collectors, but this is the Information Age, which means a bad credit rating will follow you around like a caboose many years post-graduate.

Food

Another hassle of independent living is shopping for and preparing your own food. While most colleges have a program where you can still pay for meals at the dormitory, no self-respecting upperclassman would be seen doing this.

There are two ways for roommates to buy food. One is when everyone agrees to share the costs equally and go shopping together. This works until one roommate comes home late at night with five friends in tow and eats up all the food in the house. The second way—everyone does his/her own shopping—is probably best. This way, roomie and friends have to *sneak* your food. Under this system you will find that roommates will routinely raid your half of the cupboard. In order to make it work, then, you must routinely do the same thing. Thus while everyone knows this is going on, no one will complain, as all are equally guilty.

To save money on food and kitchen items, "borrow" as much as you can while dining out. Never discard any takeout packets of salt, sugar, soy sauce, ketchup, mustard, or other condiments.

Unless you plan to live on Saltines and cold soup (which is by no means unheard of), you must learn how to cook. When you first get your own place you may entertain visions of grand feasts of cheese fondue, leg of lamb with mint jelly, and linguini with clam sauce. After a week or so, however, the more realistic peanut butter and jelly sandwich or macaroni and cheese (with, perhaps, the occasional dill pickle on the side) will become your staples. There is, however, one exception to this "no cooking" rule—the barbecue. Nothing is more essential to the apartment dweller than a mini-Weber on the porch. A few simple burgers on the grill, and—*voilà!*—even the dreariest college afternoon becomes Memorial Day.

CHAPTER 4

CLASSES

Choosing Classes

Logic would dictate that a student choose classes by criteria such as knowledge to be gained, personal interest in the subject, and relevance to the chosen course of study. There is no question that these factors should play a role in deciding what classes to take, but the experienced student also takes the intangibles into account.

Class Selection Criteria

Time

Never schedule a class before 10 A.M. A class is not a reliable reason for waking. Along those same lines, give careful thought to scheduling classes after 2 P.M. Do you really want to be sitting in a stuffy auditorium late in the afternoon when everyone else is taking a nap, outside playing ball, or mocking passersby outside the Student Union? Considerations like these tend to make 10 A.M. to 2 P.M. ideal class hours, with an hour off for lunch, of course. However, some students balk at even this schedule, as it does eliminate most of the prime tanning hours, and means soap opera nuts have to figure out how to set the VCR to tape *Days of Our Lives.*

Proximity

Proximity of your classes to where you live may not be a big deal if you attend a small college in the Sunbelt, but for everybody else, an early morning 20-minute walk through a blinding February snowstorm after three hours of sleep can really suck.

Classroom Size

Is the room big enough to sleep in without attracting undue attention? Similarly, if you arrive late can you slip in without disturbing the whole class and (more importantly) attracting the instructor's attention? On the other hand, is the class too big for effective brownnosing?

Seat Comfort

Believe it or not, many college auditoriums now offer reclining seats, especially in film and art history classes. No flight attendants or beverage service, though.

The Professor

Sure, you'll be tempted to enroll with those famous intellectuals who will actually teach you something. Every campus has a few legendary professors who are so entertaining you don't even feel like you're in a classroom.

But the bottom line is that some professors grade far more leniently than others. Even if you do the exact same work and learn the same amount, one professor may give you an "A" where another will give you a "C." Poll your friends ahead of time to find out the grading habits of prospective professors. An hour of pre-registration research in the hand is worth 20 hours of exam-time stress in the bush.

Data Bases

Find out whether anyone who has already taken the class saved their papers, notes, and most importantly, old tests. Professors may be geniuses on an academic level, but you'll be amazed at how many recycle or only slightly alter their tests and assignments from semester to semester.

Romance

What is that cute girl or guy in front of you in line at registration signing up for? Many a last-minute course selection has been made in this manner. Plus, some classes just seem to attract better-looking people (for example, Intro Psych has more potential babes than Chemical Engineering, and Shakespearean Lit dudes are generally more attractive than those studying insect morphology.)

Types of Classes

Lecture

A verbatim, monotonous reading of a textbook by a chalky, poorly-dressed, middle-aged, professor.

In college, you don't have assigned seats and you can go to the bathroom without a hall pass.

Discussion

A discussion class is smaller group meeting which usually takes place the day after a lecture. Everyone sits in a circle, just like in grade school, and again, like in grade school, the students can even ask to have class outside when the weather's nice. And just like in high school, everyone rushes to copy down answers to homework problems they didn't do the night before. A frazzled, drone-like TA (Teaching Assistant) tries to explain points that the professor rushed through in lecture. Inevitably, the entire class period is taken up by one annoying student asking inane questions.

Lab

A "lab" section implies action or active research of some sort. This doesn't always mean test tubes, bunsen burners, and long white coats, either; poetry workshops, group-marketing projects, political role-playing exercises, and Show and Tell 101 are all considered labs. Most labs, however, are excruciatingly long, technical classes in biology, chemistry, engineering, and the like. If you have enrolled in one of these more technical labs it helps to arrive early—you get a better pair of safety goggles.

Attending Classes

Attendance in some classes is not strictly required, and showing up can be a complete waste of time. Of course, when you first start school you want to go to all your classes, if for no other reason than to scope out members of the opposite sex. The key to class attendance is to get into a rhythm, to develop a sixth sense of which days will be important and which ones won't. After that first semester or two you begin to understand what kinds of information will and will not appear on the tests, and you should attend classes accordingly. Of course, you could always attend every class simply for the sheer *learning experience.*

Blowing off class every once in a while is kind of like smoking marijuana—while it doesn't necessarily lead to the hard stuff, the potential for prolonged abuse is there. You definitely want to avoid getting into that addictive "I'll go to class—*tomorrow*" rut. The symptoms are easy to spot; sleeping through lunch, sudden devotion to soap operas, and use of any possible excuse to skip class ("Kind of windy out today, isn't it?").

When you do start missing classes, you had better find reliable, upstanding people from whom to copy notes. Good penmanship is a must in these friends. If you find yourself in a bind, copy shops on big campuses often have note-taking services for certain classes. These services do tend to fleece you, though. A buck a page for class notes can cut into your entertainment money mighty quick.

Class Etiquette

- Go the first day.

- You will be issued a syllabus[2] or reading list on the first day of class. This must be lost immediately or filed away in some forgotten notebook, as you will have an unfair advantage over the rest of the students if you actually manage to keep yours.

- It is perfectly normal to sleep in class. The bigger the classroom the better, as snoozing directly in front of the instructor is frowned upon.

- If you are planning on doing the crossword puzzle in a class, either tear it out beforehand or pre-fold your paper. Even the most mellow professors have been known to fly into a rage over

---

[2] **Syllabus** (*n*) - A list of topics and books to be covered over the course of a semester. Contrary to what you may initially believe, a syllabus is a good reason *never* to read ahead. The likelihood that your class will actually cover all this material is about equal to the possibility that your final grade will be determined by your performance in a three-legged race.

the continuous sound of students folding unwieldy newspapers.

- Ever since grade school it has been taboo or unfeasible to eat in class. Remember that teacher admonishing "Did you bring enough for everyone?" Not so in college. Nothing makes an hour go by faster than a Big Gulp and a bag of Doritos. Avoid aromatic, messy foods like baby back ribs or mu shu pork, however.

- Conversation about classes is quite common in college social settings. While "cool" high school students may initially balk at such apparent social blasphemy, everybody engages in this smallest of small talk. Besides, class talk can pay off by introducing you to people whose notes you can copy, providing info on easy professors, and such. As a rule, the tougher the school, the greater the amount of "shop" talk between students. In the more uptight student bodies, "I've got so many tests coming up," has even replaced "What are you doing this weekend?" as a conversational warm-up.

- Cheating. Cheating . . . umm . . . happens. You must keep your own counsel on this matter. It is pretty easy to cheat in college without getting caught, but "scoping," as it is quaintly called, is mostly done in a limited, personal way. Cheating is certainly morally wrong, but then again, "everybody's doin' it", and why should *your* GPA (and future marketability) be sacrificed because you don't remember the key coordinates of a sine curve. Methods of cheating are limited only by

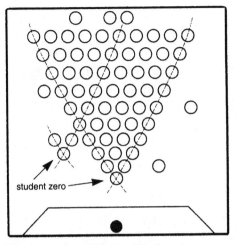

The legendary "Flying V" cheating system. Smart student up front blatantly exposes his answers to comrades sitting one row behind him to his right and left; this continues down the line each row back.

one's imagination—engineer-types have figured out ways to cheat with those complex graphic calculators that would make the CIA drool with envy. And every school has fraternities whose members get above-average grades and are thus rumored to use the "Flying V" cheating system (see accompanying graph).

• Do show up for the final exam.

The Instructor

At a private school, you may well get the kind of personalized instruction that your parents paid for. But getting personalized attention at a big university is just about impossible. At larger schools, class sizes necessitate that TAs provide part or all of the instruction.

TAs are the most technically qualified grad students the university could con into working for peanuts. Still, it's your grade on the line, so if you find yourself with a TA you can't relate to, bail out quickly and switch to another section.

Regardless of your instructor, it pays to brownnose, brownnose, and brownnose. This can't be stressed enough. In big classes, the only way to really get your hooks in is by approaching the professor for special problems, personal help, and other such matters. In smaller classes, speaking up or answering occasional questions is a must. Just don't overdo it—neither your instructors nor your classmates want to hear a "reiterator."

Computers and the Internet

With each passing semester, the computer and the Internet become more essential parts of college life. Computer work is required in quite a few courses, and even a neo-Luddite liberal arts major will need to learn how to use a word processor.

Still, this heavier focus on collegiate computer skills is nothing compared to the *real world*, where PC proficiency has become almost as necessary as regular bowel movements. Not only do you have to use computers every day in an office environment (and type pretty well, too), but proficiency with a particular word processing, desktop publishing or spreadsheet program is about the only thing that can possibly set you apart in today's job market from some tired old slob with 20 years of experience.

Today the nerve centers of both student activity and anxiety are the campus computer labs. The biggest and best computer centers are round-the-clock, utilitarian thought factories; fluorescent meccas hosting row after row of tense Windows and Macintosh interfacing, and the only sounds outside of an omnipresent electronic hum are the tap-tap-tapping of cramped fingers and the occasional Walkman turned up too loud. (Of course, half the people in the computer labs are trying to engage strangers in cybersex or searching the Web for those rumored photos of Brad Pitt naked.)

At certain points in any semester, mass hysteria ensues at these otherwise benign workplaces. Professors throughout a given university inevitably conspire to have all term papers due on the same day, ensuring that the night before, thousands of students will be scrambling to find computers. A waiting list at a computer lab during this time resembles a line at a popular lunchtime deli.

The traffic jam my be lightened up at your university of choice if you have been so fortunate as to have been admitted to one of those colleges that supply computers in the dorms. As an alternative you might want to add a PC to your Christmas or birthday list.

With increased access to computers, the Internet has replaced all meaningful social experience for a small minority of students. Do not let this happen to you. Just because your school offers you a free account doesn't mean you should use the Net 24/7. Email is great, and using the Net can be a real time-saver, but spending hours surfing the Web is not time well spent. Besides, most companies now offer their employees free Net accounts, meaning you have the rest of your life to waste downloading inane soundclips, plus you'll be getting paid for it. The exceptions to this rule are people who are not going to have a social life anyway, or those who work in the computer lab (usually one and the same).

Inevitably, these stress-filled crunch periods are aggravated by major computer crises. Perhaps a virus will run through the system, turning your eight hours of blood, sweat and bullshit into unintelligible gibberish. Or some buffoon of a janitor will plug his vacuum cleaner into the central outlet, causing a freak power outage. One must keep a Zen-like attitude towards situations like these, and budget time accordingly.

The nexus of computer crisis hysteria, however, is the dreaded laser printer. This lone ominous cube must be both respected and feared. It is the eye of the crowded computer center hurricane. Never underestimate the power of this object to jam up as you are desperately trying to print out a paper 15 minutes before class. Ancient superstition dictates that you perform some sort of ritual before printing out a major document. Ask a Comparative Religions major for suggestions.

CHAPTER 5

STUDYING

The Myths and Realities of Studying

Myth: College courses are designed to help you learn critical thinking and emphasize using your creative skills over rote memorization.
Reality: College courses are designed to emphasize your skills in creatively making it sound as if you know what you're talking about when you really haven't the slightest idea. Besides, rote memorization is at the core of most college exams.

Myth: Cramming won't help you.
Reality: Cramming is not only important, it's a way of life. You can study for most tests in two or three days. If you start a month before the test you will have forgotten

most of the material by game day anyway, so relax and pray for a mental adrenaline surge a few days before the test.

Myth: Libraries are great places to study.
Reality: Libraries are great places to socialize. They differ only from campus bars in that conversation in libraries is done in a quieter tone, and finding a needed book or reference material is easier at a campus bar.

Myth: Teachers use strict formulas to figure out grades such as midterm=25 percent, term paper=25 percent, final=50 percent.
Reality: Professors have notoriously short memories when it comes to their students, and they also love to see improvement. A good performance when professors are about to turn their grades in near the end of the semester is worth a lot more than an "A" on the first test. It's best to treat a class like a horse race—start out slow, pace yourself, and then crack the whip for the home stretch.

Myth: You should do the reading in advance to prepare for your professor's lecture.
Reality: Half the time the professor will assign readings on which you will never be tested and that will not even be mentioned in the lecture, and most professors test only on lecture material anyway. So unless you have the free time and want to really master advanced microeconomic theory, wait and read mostly to clarify lecture material.

Myth: It's no use griping about your grade, because teachers never change them.
Reality: The truth is that four out of every five times you go in to complain about your grade on a test, paper, or

final exam the teacher will change it. This is because your instructors either want to get rid of you and your whining, or they admire your resolve for actually finding their offices and putting up with their talking on the phone and chain-smoking while you sit and wait.

Myth: Copying a friend's old "A" paper will guarantee you an "A."
Reality: While this is recommended as a time-saver, be wary, first and foremost because plagiarism could result in your expulsion, and secondly because, as we stated before, an "A" paper from someone else's professor might well be a "C" paper for yours. Professors also often have graduate student "graders" handle most of the work submitted to them, which makes scores on *any* paper subject to the whims of someone you have never even seen.

Myth: Papers must be turned in at their deadline, and not a minute late.
Reality: Professors often give extensions on due dates. All you need is an excuse, and it doesn't even have to be a good one. Illness and family deaths work well for the first few papers, and after these have been exhausted the very '90s "computer excuse" never fails. Only a barbarian would try to discredit a story about a mysterious "virus" destroying not only all your files, but also the backups. Professors can't be bothered with taking the time to listen to your cockamamie story anyhow—they have corporate grants to spend. Students often *graduate* with unfinished papers.

Myth: A paper takes days to research, outline, write, edit and rewrite.
Reality: While this may be true as a freshman, you'll soon develop the skills to significantly cut down the time it

takes to complete a paper. A good measuring stick: a paper that took three days as a freshman will take three hours as a senior.

Where to Study

Choosing where to study is an art form in itself, even more important than choosing what to study. To get the most out of your study time, you must make a Zen-like peace with your environment. Studying should never be limited to just your room or a library; not only are these places incredibly distracting, but choosing them shows a complete lack of creativity. Every college offers a diverse menu of places to study; tailor your study environment to your needs at any given time.

The Library

Unless you go to school in an ant farm, you will find myriad libraries ranging from simple dormitory ones to a massive undergraduate monolith. Undergraduate libraries are crowded social havens, usually populated by freshmen and sophomores. While law and med school libraries are scholastic havens, they usually restrict entrance to law students, med students, and visiting royalty. The best bets for peace and quiet are the large yet serious business, graduate, or reference libraries. For the ultimate quiet studying experience, find your school's (*Shhhh!*) Library Sciences library.

Even in the most crowded library, you should always be able to find an open chair. In order to study properly, however, you need a *seat*. In other words, a spot where you don't have to put up with an annoying couple cooing at each other or some guy vigorously squeaking his highlighter across 95 percent of his textbook. Room to spread out, proper lighting, and easy access to emergency exits in case of disaster are all prime considerations. For obvious reasons, you should also sit as far away as possible from distractions like the periodicals section or the pay phones. Taking these variables into account, a quality seat in a crowded library can be tough to find. While the smartest idea is to find a cubicle and try to isolate yourself, be forewarned—a library study carrel somehow winds up being more comfortable than a Sealy Posturepedic, turning study time into nap time within minutes. If you tend to nod off easily, eating chocolate or applying lipstick before a study session may be prove disastrous when you fall asleep face-first on an important paper.

Your Room

Because of all the inherent temptations, your room is the absolute worst place to study. Only the most strong-willed (read "boring") students can concentrate long enough to actually study in their rooms. Most students start out with the right intentions—just gonna recline on your bed for a little while, you read better that way, right? It is very easy to rationalize studying in your room; you save the time it would take to go somewhere else, all the books and papers you may need are right there, and you can listen to your stereo and thus save the batteries in your Discman.

Studying in your room never seems to work out as planned. First you have to clean your room in order to make space for all the papers you will spread around, then you have to find that Enigma CD to study to, then the phone rings and you have to talk because it's long distance, then it's time for some caffeine and a study snack, then you decide to check your email, then your friend pops in to ask if you're going to the bar. No, you reply, you have to study, but soon you realize you've been staring at the same sentence for five minutes and it looks like a lost cause so you might as well catch your friend before it's too late. Before you know it, you are staring into a gin and tonic. Consider a study session in your room a success if you even break open a book.

Empty Classroom

Incoming students don't realize this, but most colleges keep their campus buildings open and classrooms unlocked until late at night. Empty classrooms are highly underrated as study locales, at least for underclassmen. Generally, these rooms are grabbed with uncanny regularity by study-minded students right after dinner time. If this sounds to you like a good place to find some peace and quiet, don't attempt to phone for a reservation. To reserve a room, simply get to one before anyone else, write "TAKEN" on a piece of notebook paper, and stick it on the door.

If you can get a classroom alone, you win; empty classrooms are the best places on campus to study seriously. Since a popular psychology theory says you retain knowledge best in the place you first learned it, why not use science to your advantage and study in the same room you will be tested in? Plus you get superior illumination, ample ventilation, and absolute quiet. You can also draw on the blackboard, rearrange the chairs, eat all you want, and make a general mess. After all, you don't want to put the janitors out of work, right? However, if you are studying with friends you may want to avoid this locale, as the freedom of an empty classroom usually leads to food runs every 10 minutes and/or basketball games with wadded up notebook paper.

Coffeehouse

More a place to be seen than to get anything done. If you can see your books through the haze of cigarette smoke, you've won half the battle. Usually this environment is best for studying drama, philosophy, or literature. You don't see a lot of engineers or veterinary students poring over nuclear psychics or cures for anthrax with a tall *latté* in hand. Don't forget to wear your black turtleneck.

In Another Class

Why not use your free time for the better things in life and study during other boring classes? The best classes to study in are ones where you are already buying the lecture notes, or classes you are required to attend but couldn't care less about. Avoid studying for another class, however, when there's a test going on.

Outside

When the mercury is right, the best place to study is out in the fresh air and sunshine. You may not get much done, but better to read 5 pages and catch some rays than to plow through 50 pages and retain the skin complexion of the Pillsbury Dough Boy.

In a Bar

It never fails, some geek in charge of a group project or TA trying to act hip will schedule a study session in a bar. What a kooky, nutty, crazy idea! Hate to rain on someone's parade, but you really don't look cool studying in a bar, and the only things that ever get memorized around alcohol are dirty jokes. Keep the bars for boozin' and the classrooms for schoolin'.

The Big Project

Most college courses require what is commonly known as the Big Project. On the first day of class the professor will ominously instruct you to begin thinking about this Big Project, which is always due near the end of the semester. This warning is issued to scare away those who aren't sure they want to take the class rather than to inspire prodigious work habits among the rest of the students. Some of the more idealistic professors do, however, expect their students to work on the Big Project all semester. Regardless of any unreasonable views the professor may have, only about ½ of 1 percent of the class will begin their Big Project right away so they can finish early and concentrate their studies on upcoming finals. The other 99½ percent of the class will be banging away at the keyboard the night before the Big Project is due.

While different Big Projects may be assigned for every class, they are in fact interchangeable. If you choose a topic carefully, the same Big Project may be used, with minor changes, for a bunch of different classes. For example, a Big Project on the Hearst publishing empire could be used for courses not only in history or communications, but also courses in finance (throw in a few tables with numbers), journalism (rake up some muck), political science (use the phrase *lasting implications*), sociology (the Patty Hearst kidnapping), psychology (how our thoughts are shaped by the media), engineering (how *did* they print up all those newspapers and magazines?), philosophy (just add question marks to the ends of some of your sentences), and film (*Citizen Kane*. Rent it.).

The bottom line is, no professor in his or her right mind is going to read through a couple of hundred Big Projects. Even if the professor uses a grad student to actually grade them, Big Projects are judged by a few universal criteria:

Catchy First Sentence. Busy professors will often grade a Big Project solely on the basis of the opening sentence, so make it good. For example, "Drug abuse, homosexuality, narcissism, and incest all contributed to the psyche of this most influential poet" beats "The life of Yeats sure was a real interesting one."

Bibliography. A successful Big Project must have an extensive bibliography consisting of lots of books and periodicals with important-sounding titles.

Footnotes. For a Big Project to get a big grade, even the most minor details must be footnoted. Footnote the footnotes if you must.

Visuals. Liberal use of charts, graphs, tables, diagrams, photos, and even drawings always help. Anything short of actual TV footage will be appreciated by professors or their graders; like kids, the more pictures there are, the less they have to read.

Concentrate on these aspects of your Big Project and you can't lose (unless your major is art or architecture, in which case your Big Project probably has to be three-dimensional).

The Group Big Project

Not all Big Projects are individual efforts. A creature of a different sort is the Group Big Project, where you will have to go through the torture of the Big Project with a group of randomly chosen classmates. Since you will be thrown together with complete strangers in a situation none of you wants to deal with, you may feel a general loathing toward each other. If you find yourself in a group like this, you are probably better off, since a group that gets along will waste all their time gossiping. You may at first feel that you are stuck in a group with a bunch of boring dweebs[3], but in the end you will actually be thankful.

You are also better off if your group has at least one person who is overtly anal-retentive and neurotic about grades. This person will take care of the lion's share of the work while you sit back with your feet up, spewing suggestions and wisecracks.

Usually tasks in a Group Big Project are split up because nothing but whining ever gets done when people work in groups. If you can type well, don't admit it or you are certain to get stuck with the most time-consuming job, which is typing up the entire completed project. Try and find the easiest task in the group, then make sure you whine and complain enough about it to make the others think you are working harder than they are.

Why should you care what everyone else in your group thinks of you, you ask? Well, because crafty instructors often make each member of the group turn in a secret evaluation of their cohorts, using these evaluations to grade the individual members as well as the group. Even if your professor doesn't do this, you'll probably have to contribute in some way. Most Group Big Projects end with an oral presentation in front of the class, where you have no choice but to be somewhat knowledgeable, lest your self-esteem suffer as well as your grade. Group oral presentations mean that at least two weeks of class time

---

[3] **Dweebs** (*n*) - Geeks, dorks, nerds, doofuses, nebbishes, trolls, pocket protectors et al; in other words the people who will be your bosses when you get out of college.

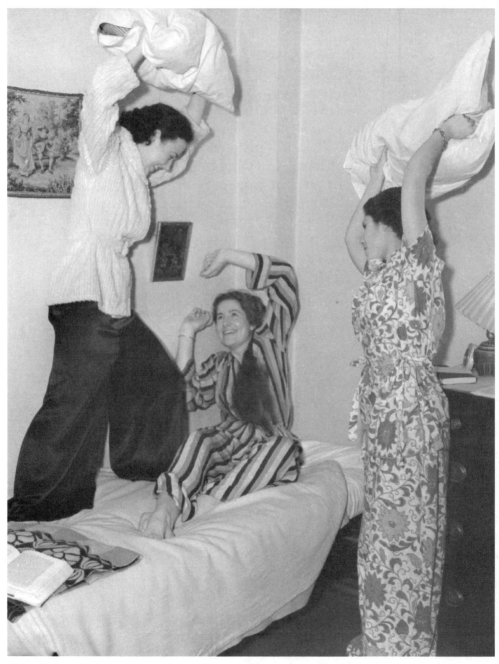

Regardless of who you get thrown into a group project with, you're sure to make new friends.

will be spent listening to them, so unless your group is scheduled to present that day, be sure to bring to class a good magazine, crossword puzzle, GameGear, or something else to study.

In actuality, the Group Big Project teaches you more about the real world than any other work you'll do in college. The lessons you'll learn about procrastinating, weaseling out of work, and convincing others to do jobs you don't want will help you in the workplace far more than any books on management or psychology will.

CHAPTER 6

MAJORS

Choosing your major is a serious decision that is either ignored or causes much unnecessary grief. Who can make career choices at age 18? Our advice is to procrastinate as long as possible. If you're lucky, your major will choose you.

At some point in your college career, most of you are simply going to have to give in and choose a major. The good news is that once you have chosen a major you are allowed—no, *expected* to change it at least two or three times before graduation. Since the only thing that matters in the end is the degree with which you graduate (and even this is questionable), feel free to use the handy chart below to randomly choose your first major.

Major	Future jobs you can get	Future jobs you can't get
English	English teacher	Anything that pays more than $20,000/yr
Engineering	All the best-paying ones	There is no job you can't get with an engineering degree
Business	The rest of the high-paying ones	Most jobs involving creativity, as artistic types scorn dronelike B-Schoolers
Fine arts	Waiter, waitress	Actor, singer, dancer, artist
Psychology	Director of Human Resources	Most of them
Biology, Physics, Chemistry	Biologist, chemist, physicist, med student	Any job requiring everyday common sense and/or functioning in the real world
Political Science, History	Grad student, panhandler	Senator, Congressman, President, Secretary of State, Secretary of HUD
Communications	Telemarketer	Ted Turner's
Physical Education	Personal trainer, gym teacher	Ones that don't require wearing a whistle
Architecture	Grad student in architecture, construction worker	Drummer for a heavy metal band
Pre-med	Doctor	Sorcerer's apprentice
Hotel/Restaurant Management	Night manager of the Comfort Inn off Rt. 16	Any job that requires less than a 60-hr. workweek
Computer Science	Game tester for Nintendo, something to do with the Internet	Fashion model
Journalist	Editor of your office newsletter	Reporter for a major newspaper
Education	Teacher's aide, substitute teacher	The good teaching jobs
Philosophy	Why are we here?	What is free will?
Foreign Language	¿Donde esta la biblioteca?	La biblioteca esta a la izquierda de Carlos.

Advantages	Disadvantages	Fun Fact
Prepared for light conversation at cocktail parties	Mocked by peers if caught reading anything less substantial than Joyce or Fitzgerald	Spend entire class periods mulling over single Faulkner sentences, yet scoff at "vacuous" business majors learning about, say, interest rates
The only students able to figure out inscrutable HP calculators	Free time bracketed around 6 hrs. of class/labs and 4 hrs. of studying daily	There is nothing "fun" about being an engineering major
Learn early how to network; spend senior year wearing interview suits	Make contacts instead of friends; spend senior year sweating in suit while friends play Frisbee	Cheat more than any other majors
Have a major that is worthwhile and meaningful	In your mind you know it's all bullshit	Anything you do out of the ordinary is considered "performance art"
Get to really understand how the mind works	Learning about psychological problems makes you realize how much of a mess you really are	Least decisive people on campus
Extremely sterile environments are perfect for anal retentives	You become skeptical while watching cartoons	Get to buy beakers, dry ice, and magnesium at educational prices
Find yourself much better at *Jeopardy!*	Unemployment gives you plenty of time to watch *Jeopardy!*	Strangely, many political science majors are completely apathetic
Learn about Marshall McCluhan	Learn about Marshall McCluhan	Biggest "fallback" major; a veritable bungee cord
Getting through school in this curriculum is about as tough as waking up every day	Waking up every day and realizing what you are actually getting a college degree in Physical Education	Friends love it when you crack their backs
A career in architecture is not only creatively rewarding, it can earn you some big bucks	Probably won't meet more than 5 non-architecture majors your entire college career	Get to make lots of cool models
When out partying, you have exact knowledge of how foreign substances will affect your body	Your understanding of ulcers won't stop you from getting one	Smell of formaldehyde tends to stick with you throughout the day
Can bring leftovers home from food preparation classes	Ruins the experience of going out to eat	A required class usually involves wine tasting
Able to figure out how to set the timer on anyone's VCR	Face it, this major doesn't bring with it a whole lot of sex appeal	Easy to get a cushy job in campus computer centers
Most journalism majors are bright, independent go-getters	Most journalism majors are arrogant, opinionated assholes	All secretly want the nickname "Scoop"
Those who cannot study, study teaching	Have to student-teach snotty kids who remind you of yourself	Get to wear Birkenstocks to work
Is nature more important than nurture?	Where is man's place in the cosmos?	Which came first, the chicken or the egg?
¿Cuantos años tiene Carlos?	Carlos tiene veintitres años.	Es un regalo para Carlito.

CHAPTER 7

GETTING AROUND

A college campus has a lifestyle of its own, one that is completely cut off from the outside world, and indeed, reality. This will be painfully obvious every time you go home from college on breaks or weekends; that place you grew up in is no longer "home" as you knew it. Your sane, normal, boring family life seems altogether surreal when compared with your college existence. At home, you may live well, eat hearty meals and drive absolutely everywhere. In college, on the other hand, you live like swine and think nothing about walking a mile and a half to get a haircut. This contrast in realities is most apparent when it comes to going places. If you don't have a car on campus, the simple act of driving will seem alien and strange when you find yourself behind the wheel of the family sedan once again during summer vacation. Although you may wonder why you need a chapter telling you how to walk or ride a bike on campus, the process is not as simple as it seems. There is a subtle art to . . .

Getting Around Campus

By Foot

Hoofin' it is still the most common way to get around on campus. College is probably the one and only time in your life you can (and will) walk everywhere you need to go. A 15-minute hike to class? Piece of cake. But would you even consider walking 15 minutes to the grocery store when living at home? People on foot own the campus—there is an unwritten law that pedestrians always have the right of way. During the between-classes rush hour, streets resemble the old "Frogger" video game, only with humans crossing the road instead of a cutesy amphibian. Students hurrying to class pay no heed whatsoever to lights or crosswalks as they blindly dart back and forth in front of frustrated motorists.

By Bike

Many students live and die by their bicycles. Literally. Psychotic cyclists think nothing of cutting through traffic on the street or navigating between pedestrians on the sidewalk. If you own a bike, don't get cocky and try to pop wheelies and ride "no-handed," as there is nothing more embarrassing than wiping out in front of a huge crowd of students on their way to class. Riding can be hazardous, but it is a lot quicker than walking. And many campuses have special paths for bikes which make riding to class both quicker and safer. If your school has one of these networks of bike paths, don't even go near them on foot, as arrogant cyclists will mow you down without remorse.

Bicycles on campus get stolen very easily, so either get a strong lock or ride a "beater"[4] that costs less than a

---

[4] **Beater** (*n*) - A vehicle that transcends normal "wear and tear" in its absolutely decrepit state of outside appearance, yet still succeeds in getting its rider from Point A to Point B.

strong lock. To deter theft some students end up taking their bikes apart at every stop on their daily routine. Carrying two wheels, a seat, and assorted derailleurs around the library can get quite cumbersome, however.

Mountain bikes are the standard, even in places like Iowa and Kansas where the biggest hill is the street curb. Bikes with curly handlebars are now the sole territory of Greg LeMond wannabes who actually pedal for exercise. Then there are the artsy types, who all have bikes which they consider cool and avant-garde. These hip machines are usually 1970s garage-sale rejects with rusty chains and banana seats.

By Moped

Mopeds are compact, energy-efficient, and can get you anywhere you want to go in a flash. And much like a good pair of shades, a scooter is not only practical but a status symbol. Owning a moped on campus is very cool, at least until someone loses an eye (scooter accidents are frequent). However, you may find a moped a bit pricey for the use you are going to get out of it, since once you leave campus having a scooter is about as convenient as having a Siamese twin. Also, watch out riding double on single-person scooters, as campus towns obtain about 90 percent of their yearly revenue from tickets campus police write for having an illegal passenger on a scooter.

By Car

Some students swear by their automobiles, using them even for short trips to class or the 7-Eleven. After a while, though, it becomes apparent that having a vehicle at school can be more trouble than it's worth, even if you do have a place to park it. Your friends will come to expect shuttle service, and if you can't or won't drive them it's no problem, they will just borrow your car. So not only are you putting an expensive vehicle at risk, but the next time you try to drive it you will be lucky to have $\frac{1}{32}$ of a gallon left in your gas tank. The sad truth is that lending out your car out at school is a no-win situation; if you don't let friends borrow your wheels you will be considered stingy, uptight, and not very nice. Avoid these automotive hassles by only using your car for trips home and keeping it a secret by parking it at a distant location, or, if necessary, covering it with camouflage netting. A distant parking location may not be by choice, however, as college towns are notorious for their shortage of parking spaces.

By Bus or Shuttle

Some campus towns have efficient mass transportation systems that take you to class or into town quickly and efficiently. Efficiently, that is, if you can decipher the bus schedules, which may prove more taxing than a graduate-level assignment in micro-biology.

By In-Line Skate

In-line skating is a very health-conscious way to get around. However, while in-line skating to class may be totally cool, sitting in class for an hour with your skates on is not. Be aware that a seething rivalry has developed on campuses between those who bike and those who skate as both groups fight for control of long stretches of smooth pavement.

By Skateboard

Way rad, dude! However, don't think a board will be as cool as it was at home. If you choose to skateboard, make sure you review your campus medical insurance policies and always carry an ample supply of gauze with you. Most people skateboarding at college are kids from the local high school taking advantage of the weird '70s architecture in front of the student loan building.

Getting From Your Hometown To College

Driving

For sheer convenience, an automobile is the best mode of transportation to and from school. Of course, you then have to deal with the mixed blessing of owning a car on campus. A new car is too expensive for the average student, so most college cars are family hand-me-downs. Your parents may give you a car to avoid the hassle of driving you back and forth to school all the time. If this happens you may think yourself incredibly fortunate to actually own a car, but any clunker your parents give you is bound to have more maintenance problems than the space shuttle, and is guaranteed to cost more in time, money, and aggravation than riding the bus or train ever would.

Then there's the matter of your sycophant friends always asking you for rides home. On the one hand it's great to have company for the ride and someone to chip in for gas, but on the other hand when friends at school say they live "near" your home they tend to use the term very loosely, usually meaning within a hundred-mile radius. So dropping someone off can easily take you an hour or two out of your way; multiply that by two or three passengers and you may as well jog home.

Riding the Bus

For most students, traveling to and from college is their first exposure to riding bus lines. It's not a pleasant experience. You will likely get stuck next to some smelly stranger in a seat that allows less comfort and maneuverability than a strait jacket. And a journey that takes three hours by car will be stretched to six by bus, with the driver making long stops every 15 miles or so to feed his face on donuts or wait for nonexistent passengers in every podunk town along the way.

This gets pretty old, pretty fast, so you must turn to time-honored coping mechanisms to relieve the stress of annoying bus rides. Alcohol (if you don't drink it, splash some under your armpits), a Walkman, and even transcendental meditation all work well, and can also clear you some elbow room. Nobody is going to voluntarily sit next to someone blaring loud, tinny music through their headphones, reeking of whiskey, and chanting "om" in the lotus position.

Mooching Rides

Mooching[5] rides from friends headed in the same direction is by far the best way to get home. It costs little to nothing, you get dropped off right at your doorstep, and you don't have any of the hassles of owning a car. The key to successfully mooching rides is to plan ahead; start asking friends who live near you at least a couple of weeks in advance. This is especially true for big holidays like Thanksgiving and winter break when there is a mass exodus from campus. Carloads fill up quickly and if you wait until the last minute it's Greyhound time.

The Ride Board

Like to gamble? Forget the roulette table and play the ride board. Every college has a ride board, usually posted in the student union or other well-traveled area. This

---

[5] **Mooching** (*v*) - Bumming, scamming, glomming, chiseling, et cetera.

You never know who you'll end up with when you take your chances
with the Ride Board.

board posts notices of people offering or looking for
rides all over this great nation. "Playing" a ride board is
about as reliable as playing with a Ouija board; the
chances that you will actually arrive at your destination
on time are all up to the laws of karma. If you're out to
meet interesting people in college, this is the way to go.
Be prepared for anything from a van full of Moonies to a
sing-along of "100 Bottles of Beer on the Wall" for seven
hours straight.

Flying Home

If you go far enough away to school, you will most likely have to fly home for the holidays and summer vacation. Typically broke college students should schedule flights with plenty of leeway time. This is because flights are often overbooked, especially around holiday times, and you may be given the option to get "bumped" from your flight, which means the airline will place you on a future flight and give you a free voucher to fly anywhere in the country. Inconvenient? Sure, but getting bumped can save you some major dough[6] and will hopefully allow your spring break in Palm Springs to be financed by the ticket your parents bought to bring you home for the holidays. Just look at the wait in the airport as a wonderful time to catch up on your reading.

"Thumbing"

Wrong decade, man.

---

[6] **Dough** (*n*) - *Cash*, baby, *cash*; moolah, bread, bones, bills, bucks, clams, cabbage, ducats, dinero, greenbacks, dead presidents—you get the picture.

CHAPTER 8

MONEY

As a college student, unless Mommy and Daddy are underwriting your every expense and extravagance, you will find yourself in a constant state of fiscal awareness (for non-business majors, this means you will always be worried about money). This chapter should show you . . .

How to Save Money in College

Stop partying.

How to *Realistically* Save Money in College

First, take into account all possible costs when estimating how much money you will need each semester. You'd be surprised at the number of . . .

Budgeting Pitfalls

Phone Costs

What does the lonely college student do upon arriving back in the room after a late night out on the town? Reach out and touch someone, of course—no matter how far away that someone may live. Things don't get really bad, though, unless your girlfriend or boyfriend studies abroad for a semester, in which case you had better either write that "Dear John/Jane" letter early or take out another student loan. While email and Internet chat can take some of the sting out of those long distance bills, nothing beats the tactile pleasures of holding a receiver to your ear.

Car Repairs

No matter how well a car ran before, when you take it to college the belt will snap, a tire will pop, a rim will bend, a hose will burst, the engine head will crack, and the axle will probably join a heavy metal band. When informing your parents of these various car problems, its best to use that serious-sounding catch-all, "it threw a rod."

Parking Tickets

Pay that $5 ticket right away, before the fine starts multiplying like well-fed amoeba in a petri dish.

Bank Fees

Was that three-burrito lunch really worth the $15 check-bouncing charge?

Dorm Fees

Don't lose your keys, as the dorm will charge outlandish amounts to let you back in your room. Also, at the end of the year buy some caulk or Gleem toothpaste to cover every single scuff and hole in your walls—this is far cheaper than the ridiculous charges for "damages" as minor as thumbtack holes.

Clothes

There is no way you're going to go a whole semester without buying a single article of clothing. Also, you had better keep an emergency fund for the aftermath of your first laundry disaster, since bleach and detergent are *not* interchangeable.

"Stick Ups" et al

Air fresheners were invented with dorm life in mind. They should be deployed anywhere and everywhere. Picture this scenario: it's the middle of winter, and three guys are living in a 10' by 20' room with two months worth of dirty laundry, stacked-up newspapers and half-full cans of Pabst Blue Ribbon piled up near the heater. Not a pretty scent, even if you're just a neighbor.

Once you have budgeted for the hidden costs of college life, it's time to take a look at your daily expenses. Think about some of these . . .

Cheesy but Honest Ways to Pinch Pennies
- 25–35 cents a day can be saved by reading used newspapers. Look for them left on desks after class or borrow your neighbors' when they're finished. If nothing else, read them in the library or coffee shop. Crossword buffs beware, though;

when you find a used paper the puzzles will usually be torn out or filled in incorrectly.

- Magazines should be borrowed from friends or skimmed[7] in the library.

- Fuel up on cheap, all-you-can-eat meals at Ponderosa, Bonanza, Sizzler, and the like—any place with a starchy food bar that stretches beyond the horizon. You may not feel well after one of these $5.99 pit stops, but you certainly won't get the munchies later.

- Potheads: get high *before* dinner, not after.

- If you have a job on campus, exploit your workplace and its resources. They're not paying you nearly enough anyway. If you work at a restaurant or fast food joint, eat as much as you are allowed. Students who work in office settings have a great place to take care of all their mail and school supplies. Employees of campus newspapers and radio stations can always find unused promotional books and discs laying around; these can be sold to secondhand stores if they're not worth keeping. Workers at campus bars—well, if you work in a bar you've probably got it figured out.

- Don't necessarily buy *all* your textbooks at the beginning of the semester. Professors are infamous for grand expectations, but they rarely cover every text on the reading list. If a particular book

---

[7] **Skim** (*v*) - To read, but not really *read*; to glom as much surface information as possible without spending too much time on in-depth analysis; in other words, MTV-reading.

doesn't seem too important, either wait to buy until it comes up in class discussion and return it within two weeks for a full refund or simply find someone in your class from whom to borrow.

Milking the P's

If, like many students, your parents are helping to put you through school, the folks have probably also come to some sort of decision about how you are to pay for your miscellaneous expenses. Generally, it goes like this: you have to pay for all your odd purchases at school, but when you're home on breaks your P's (also known as 'Rents or Units) will feed you, clothe you, give you toiletries, and often even pay for haircuts and other niceties (that Ma, what a softie!). Mom will usually do your laundry, and with a hell of a lot less wrinkles than when you throw everything in together and fill the machine way past the "full load" level.

The implications of this parental support are obvious and shouldn't have to be spelled out, but MILK THIS FOR ALL IT'S WORTH. Start hoarding supplies a good month before heading back to school. Make sure you have enough necessities to last at least a semester, and don't forget staples like suntan lotion for spring break and sheets for the upcoming toga party. Give Mom subtle hints (such as adding "one dozen packets of ramen noodles" to her shopping list). If you wear contacts, "lose" a lens or two while still at home so you have parent-purchased backups for when you inevitably tear or lose a lens.

Some coddling parents will send their son/daughter off to school with enough toiletries and foodstuffs to fill a fallout shelter. If this is the case with you, don't reject this pampering or become a survivalist, just say "thanks" and haul it all to school, hassle though it may be. Reason:

a black market fortune can be made by selling all the extra canned goods, bags of Fritos, and laxatives at cut rates to other students. Pure profit.

Parents also tend to be lenient about financing other aspects of your college life. If mom and dad haven't already offered to pay for all your calls home, you obviously haven't suggested it to them in the right manner. Likewise with transportation; if you come home for a weekend the folks should cover train, air, or bus fares home, and if you complain about the hassles of mass transportation long enough, they may even find an old car for you. It is best to try and milk the P's for big purchases like these *early* in your college stay, as parents will inevitably pamper you less and less once the "our little Pat is away at college" novelty wears off and the financial reality of how much of a drain you are kicks in.

The ATM: Giver of Life

The most important initials of your college years won't be GPA, NCAA, or even R.E.M. No, the three most revered, respected, and feared letters to any college student are *ATM*.

Automatic Teller Machines are your college lifeline. If you are scared at the thought of being away from your parents, the ATM more than takes their place. Rather than ask dad, "Can I have $10 for a movie?" you'll ask the all-powerful ATM. Unlike dad, the ATM won't question who you are going with and when you will be home, and it won't be grumpy if you bother it for something late at night. In fact, the ATM won't even care what you do with the money.

ATMs are all over college campuses, convenient when you need cash and mocking when you are overdrawn.

All this convenience comes at a cost, as banks often charge little ridiculous fees for using ATMs. Your bank may charge you a dollar for things like using another bank's ATM, withdrawing money twice in a day, or coughing while using the ATM. But if you keep an eye out for these hidden costs and leave your ATM card behind whenever you go bar-hopping, you are sure to find that this nice machine one of your best friends on campus.

CHAPTER 9

JOBS

At some point in your college career you will most likely need a part-time job to raise some extra cash or just pay the bills. The problem is, while there is work to be found on campus, good jobs are scarce. College students are cheap, abundant labor, and employers are well aware of this. Still, quite a variety of low-paying campus jobs are out there:

Dorm Cafeteria Worker
Instant employment. *Every* dormitory cafeteria constantly needs students to clean tables, wash dishes, etc. However, the prospect of doing minimum-wage drudge work, plus the fact that all your friends will be mocking you as you clear their trays in your ugly uniform with a hair net gives this job approximately the same level of prestige as being the janitor of a leper colony. And if you already live in the dorms, what good is the free food?

Pizza Delivery Person

Working as a "pizza dude" or "pizza babe" pays well, but may be the most dumped-on and potentially dangerous job on campus. Picture this typical night: at 1:30 a.m. you walk into a fraternity dressed in a pizza delivery uniform that looks like the flag of an emerging nation and get pounced on by a pack of ravenous fraternity brothers fresh from some arcane hazing ritual. You escape (untipped, of course), only to find your auto, previously stocked with hot pizzas, being ransacked by starving partiers returning from a night out. Talk about livin' on the edge! Be sure to ask if the pizza company issues you an Uzi and a Kevlar vest.

Psychology Experimentee

Big schools generally have large psychology departments, due to the astronomical number of lost souls who stumble upon psych as their major. To legitimize this curriculum and give grad students in psychology some useless statistics to mull over, psychology experiments are set up and administered on a frequent basis.

With all these tests going on, "qualified" (in other words, "living") subjects are in demand. Students in introductory psych courses are used as free guinea pigs, but most psychology departments need more subjects, so they recruit test volunteers for pay. Granted, $4 or $5 an hour isn't that great, but consider the job; playing a video game with electrodes hooked up to your chest, answering 100 yes/no questions about your childhood, looking at amorphous shapes and telling the researcher you see Julia Roberts, or something of this sort. Short of working for the government, is there an easier way to make money? Plus, years later you can look back with the satisfaction that you were a vital cog in, say, the groundbreaking study that showed an inverse relationship between memory capacity and the number of magnets on one's refrigerator. One caveat: Psychology Experiment Subject does not look good on a résumé.

ROTC Cadet

If the military is in your blood, you might as well enlist while still in college and let the government pay your tuition. Granted, marching in formation in full uniform is not the most enjoyable thing to be doing while everyone else is out having fun, but at least those little hats you get to wear are kind of cute, and there's that strange sexual fascination about people in uniform. Being a "Rotcie" is also socially acceptable nowadays, as there's no need to worry about radicals calling you "baby killer." And where else can you get college credit for firing an M-16?

Test Proctor

Sit up at the front of the hall and keep an eye on test-takers to make sure they don't cheat. Proctors are usually needed for MCAT, GMAT, and LSAT-type testing. To really enjoy this job, you need either a very vivid imagination or the ability to be entertained watching test patterns.

Fast Food Worker

While ringing up tacos or being the "#1 fry guy" may be some one's idea of a stimulating job, for the most part the enlightened college student frowns on this sort of employment. However, fast food joints are always look-ing for help, and they do give you a 50 percent discount on burgers. Pay is low but you get to meet many inter-esting members of the local populace, some of whom

Not in our list: posing for art classes can also be lucrative.

will buy one cup of coffee and sit at a table for six hours talking to themselves. And if you are lucky enough to work in a restaurant that stays open late, you can make friends with the polite, well-behaved customers who stop in fresh from a relaxing night at the campus bars.

University Janitor
The hours suck, but the pay is decent and you may be able to keep what you are doing a secret from your friends.

Sorority Busboy
Serve and clear tables for an hour or two a day during meals at a sorority. The sorority won't pay you, but you do get a free meal. Definitely a job only for guys starving both for food and for dates, and unfortunately, it usually provides only one of these in abundance.

Library Worker
School libraries are a classic collegiate workplace, containing the key student job criteria. Library employment is:

1. Easy

2. Capable of generating much slack time

3. Air-conditioned

4. Highly social

And most importantly . . .

5. Does not involve standing over a deep fryer or cash register

It is the perfect job for the intellectual; there is access to daily newspapers, magazines, and other resources, you always look busy if you're reading, and you are a cog in the great machine of knowledge. Working in a library is even more perfect for the pseudo-intellectual, second only to working in a coffeehouse. You are granted an automatic air of superiority and knowledge, and you get to use it in a very social setting (except for the uptight law and med school libraries, a stroll around a library can often be more socially rewarding than a night of laps around the hottest campus bar).

Coffeehouse Worker

Be sure to bring your attitude with you when applying for this job. Working in a coffeehouse is perfect for angst-ridden individuals who want to be seen as part of the "scene". At least 75 percent of your wardrobe should be black; earth tones should make up the rest. And don't worry—the hot, sticky, smoky atmosphere of coffeehouses ensures that employees retain their angst.

Waiter/Waitress

Without prior restaurant experience, it is tough to find these jobs on campus, since they pay well and the hours don't usually conflict with classes. If you do snag one of these gigs, the catch-22 of waiting tables in college is that the big money shifts are on the weekend nights when you usually want to *spend* the money you make. This will leave you with a lot of extra cash, but without a social life you will end up spending it on things like premium cable channels or three one-subject spiral notebooks rather than one three-subject. Also, you may want to wait on waiting tables, as this is the primary job for which most colleges are preparing their graduates.

Bouncer/Bartender

Jobs in bars are the most prestigious on campus. A bar job insures that you will be out every night, be able to drink on the job and look like a big shot setting your friends up with free drinks. Plus there's usually a late party after the bar closes. If you are beefy, thick-witted, combative, and like to sit on stools and grunt at people, being a bouncer is the job for you. And bartenders make more money than anyone else on campus. Beware, however, as a strong chance of developing a lifelong alcohol problem may be the price of a job in a campus bar.

Medical Donor/Research Subject

Some areas pay for a pint of blood. So not only do you get the satisfaction of helping your fellow man, you also get free cookies, a few bucks in your pocket, and that light-headed feeling.

Researchers also often pay student volunteers to be their subjects, and while we don't necessarily recommend doing this, it is worth noting that some members of the fledgling Grateful Dead volunteered as test subjects for LSD research in the early '60s and managed to turn it into a very lucrative career.

Telemarketer

If you can still look at yourself in the mirror every morning, these jobs pay pretty well and the hours are flexible.

Intramural Referee

Lord only knows why, but dweeby sports fanatics actually *enjoy* refereeing intramural games. Basically, intramural refs get paid about $5 a game to run around, make bad calls, and endure the abuse of people bigger and more athletic than themselves. Even if you are good at it, refereeing is still a no-win proposition: fraternity men, for example, are not known for their cool heads, and will dog the referee whenever possible on principal alone. Since college is the first time people get to participate in organized team sports without coaches or parents to keep them in check, good sportsmanship doesn't exactly run rampant. Not a job for the weak of stomach.

Fundraising Schemes

College is a hotbed of half-baked entrepreneurial ideas, some of which can actually be quite profitable. Selling T-shirts is the classic scheme, especially for those with artistic talent and cheap access to a silkscreener. T-shirt peddling is a gamble; it either leaves you with quick and easy cash or a useless pile of 500 dated shirts.

Research Assistant

Being a research assistant to a professor is usually a rather cushy position in an air-conditioned office. It pays better than the average college job, and can look great on a résumé if the job is related to your career plans. Still, it's not exactly the kind of work where you're going to meet a lot of people, and taking orders from some smelly old codger with a lot of tenure can drive even the biggest brownnoses crazy.

Resident Advisor

No longer able to boss around your younger brother or sister? Miss that assistant manager position you worked your way up to at the hot dog stand back home? Feel the urge to babysit? Becoming a resident advisor should satisfy that yearning to be an authority figure in *college*, a place where you otherwise won't be able to tell *anyone* what to do.

Copyshop Worker

Campuses are host to Kinko's and many other copyshops, so if you love collating and the smell of freshly made copies, this is the job for you. Photocopying parts of your body when bored during graveyard shifts may get you into trouble, though.

CHAPTER 10

CAFFEINE

Caffeine is a powerful and legal drug, readily available to the college student. Although the typical freshman, comes into college with the belief that caffeine is best obtained from a chocolate bar and a couple of Cokes, caffeine comes in a variety of forms.

We do not recommend the quick hitting No-Doz or Vivarin tablets, while an iced double espresso mocha *au lait* hold the whipped cream is tasty if effete. When it's time to bear down and take your place at the front lines, though, nothing beats a simple cup of java, joe, mud, sludge; i.e good old-fashioned coffee.

Knowing how to properly work up a productive "caffeine buzz" is essential to good study habits. The hardest part is keeping this "buzz" at the right level. It is all too easy to lose your productivity in a quagmire of sugar headaches, queasy stomachs, and weak bladders. Or even worse, to wire yourself up too strongly and end up a shaky, jittery, blubbering mess. Use the table below to keep an eye on your levels when getting wired.

STUDY AIDS

SUBSTANCE	CAFFEINE (mg.)	ADVANTAGES	DISADVANTAGES
Hot Cocoa	2–10	Tastes yummy!	Get real
Chocolate	25	Tastes good, easy to smuggle into library, gives placebo effect	Messy, fattening, ineffectual unless consumed in mass quantities, friends inevitably want a bite
Iced Tea	30	Socially acceptable, quenches thirst, All-American	Weak as stimulant (unless you load up on free refills), frequent urination
Tea	35	Calms the stomach	Un-American
Coke, Diet Coke, Pepsi, et al	40	Socially acceptable, tastes good, "buzz" is easy to control	Calories, sugar/sweetener headaches, tooth decay
Mountain Dew, Diet Mt. Dew	55	All of above plus a little extra kick	All of above
Anacin/Excedrin	32/65 (per tablet)	Will relieve your headache and sore joints and muscles	Pretty depressing for a stimulant
Jolt Cola	80	Pretty quick rush for a soft drink	All of above; tastes like carbonated molasses
Coffee	110	Easily obtainable, the buzz hits quickly, better establishments give free refills	Easy to miscalculate dosage, fills you up, freshmen don't like taste, adversely affects bowel movements
Capuccino, Espresso et al	100–200	Loaded with caffeine, cool with "progressive" types	A pain to make, expensive, elitist, unavailable from vending machines
No-Doz/Vivarin	100/200 (per tablet)	Instant *Bing! Bing! Bing!* pick-me-up, compact in size, won't get your fingers sticky	Socially unacceptable, easy to OD and find yourself a shaking, babbling idiot

CHAPTER 11

ALCOHOL AND OTHER CHEMICALS

The youngsters may think they partied hard at a couple of high school bashes when someone's parents were out of town, but many Americans start to drink when get to college. If you are in recovery, or alcohol is not your drug of choice, feel free to skip this chapter.

Campus Bars

Although bar scenes differ radically from school to school, certain fundamentals of campus bars are always the same:

- At least one bar on campus seems to let in pre-teenagers.

- It always takes at least 10 minutes to get a drink at a campus bar, regardless of how crowded it is.

- There is no night out like Thursday night. Thursday nights are better than weekends.

- When you are new to campus you will whine about how the doormen always let tons of people they know in line to get in ahead of you, but when you get older and know someone who works in a bar you will take shameless advantage of this.

- "House" liquors are so watered-down at most campus bars that they are hardly worth ordering, so pay the extra quarter and drink a decent name brand.

- College students rarely tip more than a spare quarter and some pocket lint.

- Then again, many campus bartenders have a hard time figuring out how to make a rum and Coke.

- Never let a shortage of funds keep you from going out, as you will somehow manage to party just as hard whether you have $5 or $50.

- Campus bars are tough places to pick up strangers, but great places to hit on people you have vaguely met but never really talked to.

- If you have the late-night munchies, leave before last call to avoid the post-bar feeding frenzy at the fast food joints.

A good fake ID is a science not to be left to amateurs.

Prescription Medicines

Every school has a student health center where prescriptions are obtained and filled. This should be milked for all it is worth. Student health centers are notoriously poorly run operations, but you might as well use them to your advantage since you pay a health fee every semester anyway. Pick up not only prescription drugs here, but cold medicine, condoms, bad advice—anything you feel you may need.

Aspirin and Other Non-Prescription Pain Relievers

Hangovers, hangovers, hangovers. A tall glass of water and a couple of aspirin before bed is one way to prevent waking up with a steel drum team practicing on your skull and a family of raccoons nesting in your mouth.

Antacids

Antacids, though often overlooked, are essential, especially with fast food/dorm food, not to mention your own pathetic attempts at cooking. Carry some at all times. The cherry-flavored ones even make tasty snacks!

Cigarettes

Although new attitudes and restrictions are inching adult smokers toward a near-leper position in society, college students are targeted by the tobacco industry trying to recruit new customers. Smoking is "in" (indeed, almost a prerequisite) with the post-alternative crowd, and is also big with crunchy granola types. Rarely will a smoke-filled room be smokier and butts be piled higher than at a meeting of an environmental group. Likewise, rarely will a room full of people be more antiseptic than at a Glee Club or School Pride meeting. Smoking is a pastime that tends to separate the artsy, liberal crowds from the school-spirit types (or in many cases the freshmen from the upperclassmen).

Things You Can't Buy at the 7-Eleven

Marijuana

While some people go through four years of school and never even see a joint, others find themselves surrounded by dope from the moment their freshman roommate unpacks his bong. For the average all-American kid from, say, Wild Rose, Wisconsin, finding his or her social life suddenly revolving around smoky, tapestry-laden rooms reeking of incense can be quite a culture shock.

Different social circles have very different attitudes regarding drugs. Many jock-types think nothing of slugging down a 12-pack of Bud, but wouldn't go near a joint of top-quality "bud." So these days the stoners, though still quite numerous around campus, keep their habits relatively private. Marijuana has proven to be a pretty harmless drug, but Nancy Reagan's decade-long PR campaign took its toll on the pot lifestyle. Don't worry though, taboos about running for public office if you have smoked a joint are being relaxed, and indeed, it is now *de rigeur* for a congressman, justice, or even chief executive to have "tried marijuana in college". And inhaling is impossible to measure, right?

Cocaine

Coke still has a (largely snobbish) following, but is fading fast as a drug of choice. This is due to its high cost, well-known health risks, and the fact that the cokehead's non-user friends tend to scatter.

POT	COUNTERPOT
Hey, if you're just sitting around watching TV anyway, why not?	Temporarily lessens constructive drive and ambition
Sit back and laugh (there goes that short-term!) when friends forget what they were saying	Tends to make one forgetful
A trip to the 7-Eleven was never this fun before	Brings on "the munchies"
Illegality satisfies need to rebel after having left home	Is illegal
That party, conversation, TV show, or whatever you were involved in was lame anyhow, right?	Tends to make one sleepy
Maybe they're right ... maybe everyone is watching you ... good thing you noticed	Can inspire feelings of paranoia
Can increase feelings of sexual response	Can increase feelings of sexual response

Hallucinogens

LSD and psilocybin mushrooms (a.k.a. "shrooms" and "zoomers". . .) have enjoyed a recent resurgence of popularity. Tripping on hallucinogens can certainly liven up college life for a weekend, but is not recommended when that Accounting 243 exam looms on the horizon. Acid is also a favorite among seniors interviewing for jobs that

Whatever you do, be sure to make time for your beauty sleep.

require drug-testing, as it is supposed to leave one's bloodstream quicker than any other substance.

Amphetamines

Speed and its offshoots, though not in widespread use, can still be found on campus. Most students who swear by amphetamines as a study aid, however, are on the 6- or 7-year plan, so draw your own conclusions.

Ecstasy
MDMA, also known as "X," "XTC," or "E" is a trendy chemical whose collegiate popularity seems to come and go every six months or so. This "love drug" makes you extremely horny and touchy/feely, so be warned before taking any if you are already hard up—you may get slapped a few times.

"Smart" Drugs
Trendy, New Age "smart" drugs are gaining popularity on trendy, New Age campuses. These drugs supposedly stimulate brain activity without any negative effects, which is all well and good, but does a Neil Young album sound any better when you are on them?

Heroin
No way.

Video Games
Video games? Drugs? Aren't they just harmless electronics? Maybe so, but Nintendo, Sega, Sony PlayStation and the like might as well be drugs for college students with addictive personalities. These games must be rationed, particularly during cold winter months when ambition is at its lowest ebb. A ridiculous amount of productive collegiate brain energy has been lost to a "just one quick game before studying" Nintendo marathon. Like anything in moderation, a reasonable daily slot of video action can be a great diversion and stress-reliever. But bring a Game Boy to study sessions and you might as well just be square-rooting your GPA.

CHAPTER 12

PIZZA

Coming out of high school, a full-fledged American *adult*, you probably think you know something about pizza. You don't. Only by leaving home and living in a college town can one understand the true spiritual meaning of pizza.

Pizza serves many important socioeconomical functions:

Pizza as *Fuel*
Cheap pizza is a life-sustaining device. Its thick, bready crust expands in the stomach (in much the same way those Sea Monkeys *supposedly* grew in water), leaving you full for hours. Cheap pizza is also a great source of energy (read C-A-R-B-O-H-Y-D-R-A-T-E-S).

Pizza as *Furniture*
Old pizza boxes become a staple of many a dorm room or apartment. These solid, ornamental works of cardboard can be used to patch up holes in walls, for mes-

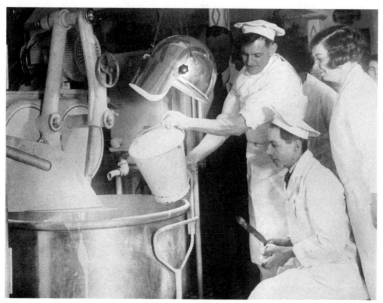

Behind the scenes at your local pizza place.

sage boards, as flatware, or as scrap paper. Stacked together, the boxes can form tables, chairs, futons, walls, ceilings/floors, or, in extreme cases, bedsheets.

Pizza as a *Come-On*

After a late night of drinkin', or even studyin', nothing beats "Hey, whaddya say we go back to my place and order up a pizza?" The combination of late-night pizza and bad cable TV can spell success for virtually any date.

Pizza as a *Leadership Exercise*

One of our most important grass-roots exercises in democracy is the group ordering of a pizza. Controlling and organizing this process has given the initial political spark to many of our most renowned public figures, from Domino's founder Tom Monaghan to General H. Norman

Schwarzkopf, who was a legend at West Point for his precision command of pizza displacement. Machiavelli himself would have a hard time with the many variables and layers of subterfuge involved in ordering a pizza for a group of hungry yet budget-conscious college students. The most crucial questions are:

How many people are in on the pizza?
Who can we cajole to chip in for this thing?

Which pizza company should we order from?
Any campus has from 3–15 different pizza dealers. You must look at factors such as: price (don't forget coupons), taste, delivery speed and reliability, sheer volume of food per pizza (the doughier the better), and extras (Free Cokes or Snickers bars? Little promotional toys? Squirt bottles?) Never ignore the extras.

What toppings do we want? Thick or thin crust?
This is often the most time-consuming part of the pizza-deliberation process. A quorum may have to be called.

How much does each of us owe?
Make the engineering or business majors figure it out.

Do we tip the pizza delivery person?
Correct answer: "Naahh" or "Yeah, round the total up so we don't have to deal with change."

It is up to you (or whoever's hungriest) to take charge of the order. If you can orchestrate this pizza process in a skillful, efficient manner, you obviously have boundless leadership potential. In other words, stay in the private sector, as you are way too marketable for government service.

Pizza as *Free Food*

When your friends or neighbors order a pizza, don't chip in for it. Wait until the pizza actually arrives and is paid for, and make sure everyone has wolfed down a piece or so. If you want to create the illusion that you aren't a mooch, don't even enter the room until the pizza is half eaten. Just hover around this feeding frenzy, and, with patience, you are sure to score. Do *not* reach in and grab a piece for yourself. This is known as *pimping*[8] *pizza*, and is frowned upon in polite company.

Early in the eating of this pizza, you must be content with just the crusts (commonly referred to as "bones"). Most people don't eat this part of a cheap pizza because the bready bones slow down consumption of the tastier parts, which means you are sure to get offered a few of these crusts. Above all, don't appear too greedy (unless there are other pizza-vultures hovering around, in which case it's every mooch for himself). Chew on a few bones and wait for an opening. It won't be long.

When the pizza gets down near the end (four–five pieces left of your basic 16" *pizza*, two or three left of a 12"), it is time to pounce. Casually mention how good the *pizza* looks and smells, and how great it would be if you could get a piece or two. By this point your friends will be happily full, and nine times out of ten will throw you whatever's left. Voilà!—a free meal. And don't even *think* of whining about how you can't stand pepperoni.

---

[8] **Pimping** (*adj.*) - Outright theft (in this context at least), and punishable as such.

CHAPTER 13

FASHION

Foreign exchange student Jean-Claude Baptiste was brought in to consult on this chapter, as it is a well-known fact that Americans are behind on their fashion tastes. For authenticity, this chapter should be read aloud in a corny French accent.

Jean-Claude's comments:

- The only rule about college fashion is that, regardless of what *Details, Vogue, GQ,* and *Rolling Stone* try to tell you, there is no such thing as college fashion. Looking fashionable in college means looking casual and developing your own identity. Spending loads of money is *not* necessary to developing this look. Most students just cultivate that "I-want-to-look-like-I-don't-care-what-I-look-like-even-though-I-spent-an-hour-getting-ready" look.

- Give your high school gym shorts and high school letter jacket to a younger sibling before going away to college. Please.

- Wearing a satiny new "U of _____" jacket makes you look just like any other middle-of-the-road yahoo[9] college freshman. Avoid blowing eighty bucks for one of these, unless, of course, you *are* a run-of-the-mill yahoo college freshman.

- If shelling out $40+ for a new double-reverse weave college sweatshirt seems a bit steep, try obtaining one from a member of the opposite sex. Many a desperate student has lowered their standards for a night in order to "borrow" a good sweatshirt the next morning. Though this may seem sleazy, an unwritten code of sweatshirt possession amnesty is universally adhered to by college students.

- Wearing a baseball hat to class is an instant sign that you woke up five minutes before class and didn't have time to shower. This is completely cool and acceptable in itself; just make sure you keep the hat on all day, lest you reveal a case of the dreaded *hat head.*

- Doing your laundry may be one of the toughest things about college life to adjust to, but it does provide an ideal opportunity to meet members of the opposite sex. The old "I'm helpless—which detergent should I use?" routine is still one of the few sure pick-up lines in the dorms. This line has

---

[9] **Yahoo** (*adj.*) - One who is *waaay* too excited about something, and frankly, just isn't cool.

a short shelf life, however, and you will pick up nothing but scorn if you try it after the first couple of months of your freshman year.

- When you live at home, you tend to think of your clothes as either clean or dirty. Things are not so simple in college. Clothes run a broad spectrum from just-out-of-the-wash to completely rancid. Judge the cleanliness of your clothes by where you are going to wear them. Going out? Clean clothes are usually in order. Going to class? Avoid noticeable stains or odors. Sticking around your room? Anything goes as long as no one complains. If a garment looks clean but smells a little raunchy, you can always apply a light coat of perfume deodorant (*spray,* not stick, dummy) before going out in public.

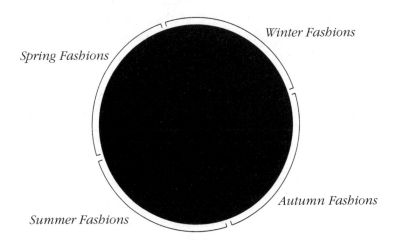

The seasonal fashion color wheel of the artsy/alternative euro style.

- Wearing sweatshirts and sweatpants with your Greek letters is OK if you are into that sort of thing, but it is far cooler to wear someone else's letters. Someone of the opposite sex's, that is. Girls love wearing fraternity letters, and will snap up any pieces of clothing they can get their hands on. Guys at some schools are considered extremely gauche if they wear sorority letters, but on other campuses the wearing of sorority letters is seen as a sign of virility. At fraternity league softball games, for example, the game itself is often secondary to the unacknowledged contest between which frat house can wear the sweats of the "best" sororities.

- Pace your T-shirt buying. College is a collection of events held for the sole purpose of commemorating them with T-shirts. Avoid obvious T-shirt themes; Snoopy shirts haven't been cool since the Eisenhower administration, and other themes arrive and become stale within a month.

  Most of these shirts feature unlicensed copying of trademarks, characters, and such, which has enraged the owners of the trademarks for decades (ask your grandfather if he still has his "Little Orphan Annie getting drunk" T-shirt). An original, obscure T-shirt is a great conversation piece, especially if you are the first kid on the block wearing it. An instantly stale fad shirt, however, carries a stigma worse than parachute pants.

- If you do get caught wearing something of questionable fashion taste (Cheryl Tiegs-brand jeans, edible or day-glo underwear, "floods," etc.), turn it to your advantage by pretending you are wearing it to show off your ultra-hip, retro-ironic sense of style.

Note of warning to readers: after the manuscript was completed, it was discovered that fashion consultant Jean-Claude, though certainly a foreign-exchange student, actually hails from Canada.

Developing your own style is the key to being fashionable in college.

CHAPTER 14

SOCIAL LIFE

Social Types

Yeah, yeah, college is a place of individuals, and a place to get in touch with one's own individuality, blah blah blah. But as it is the first time most people live away from home, they tend to get influenced by their newly-made friends, and soon place themselves in easily-defined categories:

GENERIC COLLEGIAN

Fashion: Polo, Champion, and Ray Bans, always Ray Bans

Food: McDonald's, McDonald's salads

Recreational
reading: Stephen King, V.C. Andrews

Music: *Eagles Greatest Hits (Vols. I and II),* Pearl Jam's *Vitalogy*

Movie: *Fletch, Speed*

Creed: "Oh, you're from _____. Do you know _____?"

EURO-PREP

Fashion: J. Crew catalog

Food: Anything served at a café

Recreational
reading: *Gravity's Rainbow*

Music: Morrissey, Oasis

Movie: *Before Sunrise,* anything with subtitles

Creed: "Hand wash separately as colors may fade"

COMPUTER CENTER FIXTURE

Fashion: Garanimals

Food: Orange Crush, Mike & Ikes, Andy Capp Hot Fries or whatever's left in the vending machine

Recreational
reading: *Unix Made Easy, Internet Underground*

Music: Aphex Twin, Prodigy

Movie: *Star Trek, Star Trek II, Star Trek III . . .*

Creed: "You may now switch off your Macintosh safely"

GRANOLA

Fashion: Birkenstocks, anything made in Guatemala

Food: Brown rice, tofu, veggie pasta

Recreational reading: *Zen and the Art of Motorcycle Maintenance*

Music: Rochester 3/17/85 (II)

Movie: *Dazed and Confused*

Creed: "Hey, now"

SLOB

Fashion: Sweats, baseball cap

Food: Pizza, leftover pizza

Recreational reading: Marvel Comics, *The Catcher in the Rye* until he finds out it's not about baseball

Music: Van Halen, ESPN's Jock Jams

Movie: *Animal House, Caddyshack*

Creed: "Who's in for hoops?"

PRINCESS

Fashion: 2-piece tie-dye outfits, sweats with rhinestones

Food: Diet Coke, pita bread, frozen yogurt

Recreational reading: Danielle Steele, *Elle*

Music: *Best of the Grateful Dead, Cracked Rear View*

Movie: *Ghost, Beaches, Terms of Endearment*

Creed: "Oh my Gawd!"

CORPORATE CLIMBER

Fashion:	*Wall Street Journal* tucked under arm
Food:	Power lunches
Recreational reading:	*In Search of Excellence, The Art of War*
Music:	Subliminal motivational tapes
Movie:	*Risky Business, The Secret of My Success*
Creed:	*"E Pluribus Unum"*

Parties

Although increased alcohol awareness coupled with local and university restrictions have toned down campus partying in the last few years, college is still a good place to go to parties.

Attending Parties

It is best to go to parties with a relatively large group of friends so as to have a cushion of people to fall back on when companions inevitably get tired, go home with someone or disappear upstairs to "mash,"[10] make phone calls, do drugs, or some other private endeavor. This is especially true for women, who even this late in the century are better off finding safety in numbers. However, anyone party-hopping with a big wolfpack can also find it socially inhibiting; you will invariably spend the whole time with the people you came with, making fun

---

[10] **Mash** (*v*) - To "make out"; smooching and beyond, all the way up to a hazily-defined point when things become a little more serious than a mere *mash*. This point depends entirely on who you are talking to, how you really feel about the person you mashed with, how dark it was, how embarrassed you are about it, how worried you may be about your reputation, and whether or not it's anyone else's business.

of others and just being generally negative. If you actually want to meet new people and do not fear the unknown, try walking into a strange party alone or with just one friend.

The Keg

College parties center around the keg[11] (or a trough full of beer if your oppressive college doesn't allow kegs). Knowledge of keg etiquette is a must, as the keg and the area surrounding it have unique rituals and customs that must be observed.

Finding a cup. Hard as it is to imagine, your hosts might not be providing free cups. Since it is a mortal sin to spend even a few unnecessary bucks in college, before paying for a cup try having an attractive-looking friend attempt to obtain one.

Getting a beer. Assuming that the person pouring the beer is male, a definite order determines who gets beer first:

1. Persons throwing the party

2. Distinguished guests

3. Buddies of person pouring beer

4. Women known to person pouring beer

5. Brawny, pushy jock-types

6. Women the beer-pourer wishes to know

---

[11] **Keg** (*n*) - The big kettle-shaped thing that holds the beer. If you have had to read this footnote, you have a long way to go . . .

7. People who look vaguely familiar to beer-pourer

8. Any other women

9. Patient guys who seem pretty cool

10. Other guys, but only if they're directly in front of the tap, have been waiting longer than 10 minutes, and none of above are back for a refill

The Crowd

Walking with your drink. Navigating a crowded party without spilling your drink on someone is a skill worth mastering. It's all too easy to lose your beverage on some stranger's shirt. Generally, a mixed drink with lots of ice is the best bet for safe transport, since at crowded parties beer tends to slosh.

Making conversation. It is easy to find yourself at a loss for anything intelligent to say, especially when you hardly know the person you're talking to and feel as big as a woolly mammoth. And chatting about the weather just doesn't cut it at 2 a.m. in a crowded party with a live band cranking in the background. The best bet is to bring up mutual friends or the possibility of them ("Do you know _____?") If this has been exhausted and you absolutely can't think of *anything* else, fall back on talking about classes. Just keep in mind that *nobody* cares how many tests you have coming up and how you haven't even started studying for them.

Avoiding unwanted conversation. Getting stuck in long conversations with people you could care less about can be a big problem. A surefire way out of this is to always carry an extra cocktail in your free hand so that you can say "Excuse me, but I have to bring my friend his drink," and thus extract yourself from a boring conversation.

Proper timing is a key element in throwing a successful bash.

Throwing Parties

Most dormitories have alcohol policies that are tighter than the choreography in a Janet Jackson video, so you probably won't get a chance to show your party-throwing skills until you live in a house or apartment. When you do, be sure to take the following variables into account:

Timing. Proper timing is a key element in throwing a successful bash, especially in today's study-conscious college days. Except for the first few weeks of a semester, a party will rarely work on a Monday or Tuesday, so it's best not to even bother throwing one these nights. Similarly, *everyone* throws Christmas, Halloween, and St.

Patty's Day parties, so unless you have a solid network of friends to rely on your bash may be a bust due to competition. To escape this holiday party glut and make the event more memorable for everyone, throw parties on more obscure occasions, such as Arbor Day, Groundhog's Day, or National Smoke-Out Day. If no holiday is in sight, you can always use a theme like Casino Night, Seventies Revival, or "Man Is Inherently Evil." All work well, especially the latter in Joseph Conrad's *Heart of Darkness.*

Promotion. Remember what a hit your third grade birthday party was? Did people find out about it through word-of-mouth? The rumor mill? Nope. The party was a success because you gave out *invitations.* Invitations are as simple as finding a computer with a variety of fonts, throwing them all together in a vaguely witty manner, running off 100 or so at Kinko's on funky-colored paper, and passing them out a week before the party.

What to serve. Beer, of course, is the traditional college-party fare. We recommend that you buy the cheapest available, preferably in a keg. You, however, will hide your own beverage of choice in the back of the refrigerator behind last week's leftovers.

A beverage alternative can also help keep the partygoers lubricated. Punch works well, and it needn't taste good. Help out your non-drinking friends by serving seltzer as well.

The aftermath. There will be some degree of cleanup involved so be fully prepared the next morning to purge your place of the inevitable Eau de Stale Busch. And never forget that half the fun of throwing a party is the next-day recounting of who showed up, who you wish hadn't shown up, who said they'd show up and didn't, who left with whom, who you and your roommates ended up or struck out with, who was looking good, who wasn't, and where did that horse's head come from and how did it get on top of the TV, anyway?

Parents' Weekend

Every college has a special weekend for parents to come to campus, get shocked by their son/daughter's living conditions, and donate money to the university, their children's Greek house or other organization, and most importantly, their children themselves. Even the most independent college students should note the advantages of the P's coming down for a night or two:

- Delivery of home-baked food. Hide immediately from roommates.

- New clothing and other supplies. Hint: a trip to the local mall can be a great way to kill an afternoon with the folks.

- A ticket to the football game and maybe even a hot dog or two.

- Free lunch, dinner, and maybe even breakfast the next morning. Order extra, take it back in doggie bags, and you should be able to feed yourself until Wednesday.

Parents' weekends also provide a great opportunity to let your folks see you in your new environment, giving them a chance to adjust to the "adult" you.

CHAPTER 15

DATING

Depending on one's perspective at any given moment, dating is either the single most important thing in college or the biggest nightmare. Obviously you must follow your own instincts when it comes to your libido, so all we ask is that you just try and pay heed to a few caveats.

Collegiate Dating (or, Sex, Lies, and Video Rentals)

At most colleges, there is a definite lack of the old-fashioned call-someone-up-and-go-out-for-a-malt kind of date. Groups of people go out, and maybe a couple will pair up and scam on each other one night. After this, they *may* start going out on dates. Everyone complains about this stilted, group-oriented dating procedure, so you may want to score some points by getting radical, picking up a phone, and asking someone out. Of course, it may be tough finding a malt shop to go to, so you'll just have to suggest a creative alternative.

First Dates

Avoid taking a first date to a place where your friends hang out. You will either spend the whole date talking to your friends and annoying your date or talking to your date and later enduring the wrath of your friends. The situation is awkward enough as it is. Besides, nothing is more embarrassing than running into a bunch of your drunken friends while trying to impress a date.

Dinner is not always a good college first date. Too much money to blow on a potential disaster. Plus no one likes to show off eating habits.

Movies are a useful tool for reluctant first dates, as little-to-no conversation is involved. If the two of you are getting along you can go out afterwards and, if nothing else, discuss the movie you just saw. To show off your hipness, take your date to an old movie or cult film; this can also serve to help you determine the intellectual capacity of your date.

Under no circumstances take a first date to a:
- Dorm cafeteria
- Screening of *Deep Throat*
- Scientology workshop
- Speed-metal concert
- Chili cookoff
- Fish hatchery
- Self-wash car wash
- Off-track betting parlor
- Monster truck rally

Extended Dating

The key to extended dating is to get things past the "dinner and a movie" stage as quickly as possible, because it can be very expensive. Once you are truly *dating,* home-cooked pasta, rented movies and (safe) sex will do quite nicely. College is also a great place to try offbeat, juvenile things on dates. Impress your date by showing off your fun-loving sense of abandon in the high-pressure world of college with activities like apple-picking, playground picnics, flying a kite, or Twister. Or try the intellectual rap and suggest an art museum, a play, a philosophy lecture, or just sitting at home by candlelight translating copies of the Dead Sea Scrolls.

The Relationship

Dating for more than a month in the fast-paced world of college means that you have entered a *relationship.* You and your boyfriend/girlfriend will begin spending enormous amounts of time together, and will end up living out of whichever room is bigger.

College relationships can get pretty sappy rather quickly as they begin, and can end just as quickly, so pay heed to a few words of advice:

- Try not to totally blow off the rest of your friends for your new boy/girlfriend, as you will need friends when the axe does come down.

- If your relationship goes past six months, be prepared to forever be associated with your significant other. Even if you break up, people will see you and ask "How's Susie?", "Do you still talk to Susie?", or even worse, "Would you mind if I asked Susie out?"

It's not always wise to jump right into the first relationship that comes along. There will be other chances.

- Don't buy things "together". This can end up as bitter as a divorce; "I bought that CD", "Gimme back my toaster oven", "That six-pack is half-mine," and so forth.

- As much as it may make sense considering that the two of you spend 23½ hours a day together, don't take the big step of officially living together. At college you need a place to retreat even if it's just for a half-hour a day to watch *Jeopardy!* or work on your photo album.

- If you are in love it's OK to be affectionate in public, but control the tendency to be nauseatingly lovey-dovey. Avoid spectacles like holding hands while studying in the library, feeding each other lunch in a crowded hot dog place, or having your lover's name tattooed on your body (at least on plainly visible parts).

- Pace the gift-buying for each other. Start slowly and stay within a college budget before gradually working your way up to big-ticket items. Perishable goods like heart-shaped cookies or bottles of wine are good starters, as are cheap items of sentiment, such as homemade mix tapes, small teddy bears, or economy packs of condoms. A framed photo of yourself is a versatile gift; it can be reused if your lover throws it at you when you break up (provided you catch it, of course).

- Try not to associate sentimental things about college with your relationship, because when you are older, instead of smiling and sighing "that song reminds me of college", you will mope as the song reminds you of that lost love. When you go back for Homecoming, the simple act of getting some food will make you sad—"that was *our* pizza joint." Nothing makes memories of college more depressing than the realization that you spent the best four years of your life in an obsessive relationship that went nowhere, so be sure to cultivate some fond remembrances of college apart from things you did with your significant other.

Scholastic Sex Advice

If on the off chance you do get lucky and take that special someone back to your dorm room, you will need to work out a system with your roommates so they don't interrupt your amorous rendezvous. Subtlety is the key; a flashing siren, road flare, or neon "I'm Getting Some!" sign, while effective, will only draw unwanted attention. Try a piece of masking tape on the doorknob.

If you *must* have sex in your dorm room while your roommate(s) are trying to sleep, limit yourself to discrete positions and keep the rustling of sheets to a minimum. Do the honorable thing and take your roomie(s) out to breakfast in the morning.

Having a hard time finding a date for a party? The old "out of town" date, though a bit of a cop-out, can be your best bet. This category includes someone you dated in high school, a scam that goes to a nearby college, that person you had a fling with over break, and the like.

Many colleges distribute condoms free to students at their health center. Not only does this save you lots of money, it's always fun to go home that first Thanksgiving break, throw a big sack of rubbers on the floor, and say "Look, Ma, they pass these out at school." Even if you aren't fortunate enough to get large quantities of condoms free at your school, we shouldn't have to tell you that it's a good idea to put a helmet on that soldier. Women, don't count on men to carry condoms: make sure that you have a drawerful. It will save you from having to listen to lame excuses.

Best Times To Scam On Members Of The Opposite Sex

- Think about making your moves right at the beginning of the semester, before classes kick in and everybody latches onto the best thing available and settles down in a relationship.

- Most schools have a weekend in the summer when students go back to campus to party. This is an ideal time to pounce: everyone gets bored and lonely during summer vacation at home, and loves to let go for a weekend on campus. Just be sure you have a place to go if you do pick up someone.

- When visiting other campuses. Why? First of all, who cares if you strike out? It's not as if you'll run into the person around town. Secondly, someone looking for a one-nighter will latch onto you because they figure their reputation is safe with a person from out-of-town. If at a loss for an opener at an unfamiliar campus, you can always use "Didn't I talk to you in line at the copy shop last week?" as *every* campus has a copy shop.

- At work. If you need some new scenery in your life, get a job on campus, preferably one where there's lots of time to talk to attractive co-workers about how much you both hate working there.

- In classes, believe it or not, as long as you don't use lines that are *too* cheesy, such as "Can I borrow a piece of paper . . . *with your phone number on it?*"

- Generally, between the hours of midnight and
  1 A.M., and again, at late parties, during the
  "picking up the scraps" hour of 3 A.M.–4 A.M.

- On spring break. 'Nuff said.

THE WALK OF SHAME

The walk of shame takes place between 5 A.M. and noon on the morning after an overnight liaison, or "shack," with a member of the opposite sex. If the "shack" has taken place in a house, this walk begins as you slink down the stairs praying no one else in the house has gotten up yet. Note that a walk from a boyfriend/girlfriend's place is not "of shame"— the trek must take place after a more casual sort of fling. The truly "shameful" walk takes place after a one-night stand.

Characteristics of the "shamewalker":

- Skewed, slightly secretive smile *or* skewed, slightly regretful frown

- Walking alone, always alone

- Disheveled, often formal clothing

- Matted, messed-up hair

- Glazed eyes, bags under eyelids

- Ducks in back entrance of dorm/house/ apartment building

CHAPTER 16

ACTIVITIES

"Get involved", "Be a part from the start", "Join in the fun." Et cetera. Clichés all, and annoying ones at that. Still, much as we hate to admit it, The Man is right this time—a healthy dose of extra-curricular activities is essential to a successful college career. College is too open an environment for one to limit oneself to just studying (or drinking, or procrastinating, or "finding yourself" or whatever your reason is for going to school). And while in a perfect world, collegiate activities would be participated in for their sheer enjoyment or experience, the reality is that the more things you do and people you meet while in college, the better your career network and social life will be in the real world.

Why Join Activities?

To put them on my résumé
Gooooood answer! Four out of five students surveyed prefer jobs to panhandling when they graduate.

Because they interest me
Another popular and certainly valid reason. Kinda says something scary about people who join the Accounting Club in their spare time or wave flags for the marching band in starchy costumes during 95 degree heat, though, doesn't it?

To meet more people
And meet people you will. If you find an organization you really like, you may even find your other friends complaining "He's blowing us off again for his Horticulture Club buddies" or "She's too good for us now that she's president of the Society of Women Engineers".

Because my best friend just did
It's important to have an ally in an organization, if only to have someone to help you make fun of the other members of the group. Be wary of how far you take this, though, for nothing is worse than two friends who join an organization and then isolate themselves from the rest of their friends because they decide anyone who's not in, for example, the Ham Radio Club is a nobody.

Because its nice to be able to tell people, especially your parents, that you do more with your free time than play computer games and watch TV

Why Haven't You Joined Activities?

Fear of the unknown

A lame but touchingly human reason. To get over this fear, either: a) slug down a couple shots of Jaegermeister before your first meeting to loosen yourself up, or b) convince yourself that attractive members of the opposite sex will be in the organization (granted, this can be tough if you are looking to join the Star Trek Appreciation Society).

"I don't have enough time"

This reason is only valid if you have to work full-time to pay for your education. Otherwise, lack of time is a pathetic excuse used mostly by sniveling study-mongers. You know the type, the ones who need a 65 on the final to get an "A" in a class, yet study for three days straight anyway. A true college education consists of a hell of a lot more than just nights filled with needlessly stressed-out study sessions. There's no reason not to sign up for an activity or two; belonging to one usually requires less than five hours a week of your time, most of which consists of eating free donuts.

The activity doesn't seem "cool" enough

In some cases (the Glee Club comes immediately to mind) this is a valid reason, but generally, the people who will be interviewing you for your future job will *not* be members of your fraternity or sorority, and probably won't share your definition of "cool," so perhaps it's time to learn how the other half lives.

Fear of rejection

Many of the more desirable activities require tryouts, which means there's a good chance that you won't make the cut. The bottom line is that to "make" a group, you need to politic and schmooze like never before, which teaches you more about the real world than most other aspects of your college experience will. Rather than get depressed when you get axed, think of it as a "learning experience" designed to give you the steely will and stoicism needed to compete in the postgraduate job market . . .

Because all you really enjoy is partying and watching TV

What You're Getting Into When You Join

Student Government

Duties: set agendas; pass meaningless resolutions; learn ins and outs of Robert's Rules of Order; rant; rave; condemn third world dictatorships; enforce political correctness

How to run for student government:

1. Speak passionately about minor issues to small groups of apathetic students who are either: a) forced to listen to you for a political science or speech communications class; b) covering the event for the school paper; or c) your opponents

2. Always keep in mind that getting your roommate to vote for you will probably be enough to get you elected no matter what size your school is

3. Whether you win or lose, demand that the ballots be recounted

Typical member qualities: High-strung, self-important, living in own world

Political Organizations
(i.e., Campus Republicans, Croatian Student Activists, Coalition to Boycott Bottled Water)

Duties: Know the ins and outs of selling organic foods to raise money; hone leadership abilities, since chances are you will be the president, premier, czar, big cheese, or at least recording secretary of any group you are a part of

Typical member qualities: Unnatural passion for obscure causes, absence of anything else remotely worthwhile in your life, furrowed brow

Student Newspaper
Duties: Believe misguidedly that students read the campus paper for anything but the classified ads, entertainment listings, and the comics; argue with editor over earth-shattering issues such as when to use "who" or "whom"; cover fascinating topics like local zoning ordinances, meetings of the Students for Guam Statehood, and yes, student government elections (see previous entry)

Typical member qualities: Desire to spend all free time with social misfits with whom you work on the paper, desire to use said time arguing about trivial issues with these same people

The Student Union

Every campus has a building enigmatically known as the Student Union. Many students avoid this building when they first arrive on campus, worrying that if they enter they may have to pay dues and march in picket lines from time to time. They soon realize, however, that the union is a treasure trove of cool and occasionally useful services and activities. At most schools, especially the bigger ones, you can spend an entire day at the union and stay entertained the whole time. Where else in the known world can you:

- Cash a check
- Start the day off with a cold one at the bar
- Adjourn to the lounge to recline and attempt to study on a Victorian couch
- Shoot a game of 8-ball, and follow it up with some multi-level pinball
- Use the rest room
- Browse through magazines worth reading but not subscribing to
- Hobnob with members of your student government (both of them!)
- Seek counsel at the Student Legal Service office
- Buy tickets to the upcoming student production of *Cats*
- Wait impatiently for a friend who was supposed to meet you 5 minutes ago
- Type your four-page paper on the Irish Potato Famine at the computer lab
- Book a bus ticket home for Thanksgiving break
- Bowl a few frames
- Grab a pickle-on-a-stick at the snack bar
- Wash it down with a sip of water at a drinking fountain
- Mull over the pretentious, tortured paintings exhibited in the art gallery
- Light up a cigarette to help replenish the constantly smoky air
- Hold a placard in a pro-choice rally
- Sleep the night away in a private room upstairs

Note: some activities may not be available at your school. Consult your local union for details.

Yearbook

Duties: Change wording slightly from last year's yearbook; write inane captions for human-interest photos; focus yearbook on activities of dorky yearbook editors like yourself; squeeze in photos of friends wherever possible

Typical member qualities: Nostalgic, cursed with poor writing skills

Marching Band

Duties: Prance around in silly, unwashable, polyester/rayon-blend uniforms; practice for 30 hours a week to play Henry Mancini salutes at half-time to oblivious alumni while students go to concession stands; aspire someday to be the member who gets to wear that ridiculous, frilly, Grand Poobah-esque hat

Typical member qualities: Overweight, prone to acne, band member in high school

Glee Club

Duties: Sing; cultivate handlebar mustache; bastardize popular songs

Typical member qualities: Glee, voice

Campus Radio Station

Duties: Play obscure music that is almost impossible to enjoy but really makes a statement, or better yet, makes a statement by not making a statement; show disdain for Bon Jovi at all times; cultivate loyal listenership of three or four people

Typical member qualities: Large yet incredibly narrow music collection; belief that vinyl is not yet dead

CAMPUS POLITICS: POLITICAL NEGLECT

Regardless of media hype about a new student activism, today's college students just don't care that much about politics. For the average student, complaining about parking restrictions or listening to Rage Against the Machine disc is about as political as it gets.

Still, a small but growing percentage of students on any given campus are politically active. Unfortunately, every single one of these students is fervidly devoted to some fringe cause, whether it be on the far left or far right. These are the students who build shanties, spray-paint "STOP PANTYHOSE" all over sidewalks, conduct candlelight vigils, hang the university president in effigy, listen to "world beat" music and write all the letters to the editor in the campus paper.

The same students make up the body of every campus political demonstration.

The main result of these demonstrations is to give the campus newspaper something other than sports reportage to fill its pages. Occasionally a well-run protest may even pick up some local and/or national TV coverage.

Political correctness is a controversial development that affects nearly all college campuses. You'll have to determine for yourself the level of correctness of your own student body.

THE POLITICALLY CORRECT STUDENT	THE POLITICALLY INCORRECT STUDENT
Major: Environmental Studies	Major: Military Studies
Uses inclusive language: • "Freshman" becomes "first-year student" • "Policeman" turns into "police officer"	Uses lots of swear words
Boycotts all the right products	Actively buys boycotted items in bulk
Refers to all females, no matter what age, as women	Refers to females as "chicks," "babes," "Bettys," or "broads"
Weekend agenda includes rallies, candlelight vigils, workshops, and sit-ins	Weekend agenda includes renting porn movies, hunting, and littering
Favorite writer: Virginia Woolf	Favorite writer: Tom Clancy
Eats falafel	Can't pronounce falafel
Wears burlap, anything scratchy	Wears sable coat, alligator-skin boots, anything endangered
Drinks herbal tea	Drinks malt liquor

Student Alumni Association

Duties: Suck up to prominent alumni to raise money for school; enjoy trips, parties, and other university-paid perks in pursuit of this

Typical member qualities: Nice smile, all-American look

Literary Magazine

Duties: Pour your soul into writing for a compilation that will sell about 50 copies out of sympathy and will actually be read by, at most, a couple of sympathetic, masochistic English professors; attempt suicide at least once during college career; if editor, flog your way through pages of horrible prose in hope of finding hidden jewels; host "big" publishing party at hip campus coffeehouse

Typical member qualities: Angst, lack of actual literary talent, large collection of depressing music

Medieval/Wargamers Societies

Duties: Wrongly glorify a dark period of history; participate in yearly "joust" in center of campus; blow spending money on dice, metal figurines, or costumes; refer to beer as "mead"

Typical member qualities: Vivid imagination, bad facial hair (male or female), product of inbreeding

Theatre

Duties: Hold on to misplaced belief that acting in plays is a viable route to stardom in these days of Arnold Schwartzenegger, Sylvester Stallone, and Sharon Stone; encourage parents to come down for the weekend so they can see you utter two syllables in a bit role

Typical member qualities: "Sensitive" nature, manic-depression

Without cheerleaders, "The Wave" as we know it might have faded into extinction.

Cheerleading/ Pep Squad

Duties: Wear wholesome uniform; interact with school mascot; provide pre-commercial break "pep" for nationally televised games

Typical member qualities: Pep, low IQ, good teeth

Volunteer Organizations

Duties: Aid homeless; provide peer counseling; participate in community mentoring programs; clean up neighborhood

Typical member qualities: Guilt

Karate/Tae Kwan Do Clubs

Duties: Try for a semester and quit, keeping nice robe as souvenir; "Great workout, but I just didn't have the time"; years later, remember basic moves enough to drunkenly demonstrate at parties

Typical member qualities: Intense, brooding loner-type grad student (then again, are there any grad students who aren't intense, brooding loners?), hero-worshipper of Steven Segal, Jean-Claude Van Damme, and Kung Fu

School Mascot
Duties: Wear 90 lb. woolen costume on 115 degree field; get attacked by opposing cheerleaders who pretend to ram you crotch-first into goal post to delight of sold-out crowd

Typical member qualities: Fit into mascot costume, harbor secret desire to be next Philly Phanatic

Hobby Clubs
(i.e., Model Airplaners, Bridge Club, Sherlock Holmes Society)
Duties: Bond with people with similar inane and/or arcane pursuits

Typical member qualities: Lonely childhood, poor social skills

Key Clubs/Campus Tours
Duties: Represent school; show parents and prospective students around campus; do other nice, helpful chores for university

Typical member qualities: Upwardly mobile, overbearingly friendly, know way around campus

Orchestra
Duties: Practice long and hard

Typical member qualities: Who knows? Does anybody actually know somebody in the college orchestra?

CHAPTER 17

SPORTS

Intramurals

Intramurals provide the best post-high school sporting action this side of corporate softball leagues. Collegiate intramural sports can get very competitive. This is especially true in the frat leagues, where disgruntled ex-high school jocks are not only extending their personal "Glory Days," but are also playing for the very honor of their hallowed fraternal institution. Whatever. At any rate, intramurals are:

Fun For Everyone!
Even the biggest misfits can find intramural activities at which to excel. Bowling is big with stoners. Loners and grad students dominate the racquetball leagues. Swimming and water polo clubs abound for those who miss

the Speedo bonding of their high school teams. Billiards or even euchre[12] are favorites with couch potatoes or brainy nebbishes.

Newsworthy!

Believe it or not, most campuses have someone who covers the intramural leagues for the school paper. This is invariably some geek trying to work his way up to a column in the sports section so he can rag on the football coach every week. This hard-hitting coverage has a small but loyal readership consisting of a) the people who played in the game themselves, b) the rival teams with games coming up (for scouting purposes) and c) the girlfriends of the people who played the games themselves (after their boyfriends have told them to look in the paper).

Sources of Lively Wardrobe Additions!

Intramurals give you the chance to have cheap T-shirts printed up that identify you as a teammate (7th Floor Huber Cheetahs!) with all the other dweebs on your dorm floor.

Pickup Hoops

For guys, pickup games of basketball are the choice for college recreation. The late afternoon hours are prime time for hooping, and classes must be scheduled accordingly. College resembles grade school in that the kid with the basketball suddenly finds himself with lots of friends. If you do bring a ball to college, be prepared to

---

[12] **Euchre** (*n*) - Some card game that neither of the authors of this book ever understood.

hoop religiously, as people are going to constantly borrow it, and playing in every game yourself is the only way to ensure you hang onto it.

Other Recreation

Not everyone is into using competitive sports to knock off that "freshman 15," so campus recreation centers at most schools provide plenty of other machines, devices, and classes to serve as an excuse for wearing leggings and spandex. There are Nautilus machines, Universal machines, Lifecycles, Stairmasters, Rowmasters, Lug-20 lb.-Blocks-of-Ice-on-Your-Back-for-Four-Miles-Masters, and even a few square feet of carpet where you can do archaic exercises like pushups or sit-ups.

The best thing about these recreation centers is that, unlike the real world, you don't have to pay $40 a month (not to mention that $150 one-time "initiation fee") to work out in some cheezy, neon/pastel money trap of a health club. Of course, running and cycling are always exercise options for anti-social, outdoorsy, hard-liner types.

College Football

Do you find it tough to support your team with all your heart without knowing exactly what you are cheering for, or indeed, whether you are even applauding at the right time? Do you yearn to understand the game? To feel that adrenaline rush every time you see an opposing player flattened by your middle linebacker? To relish the sound of shoulder pads and helmets colliding and cracking with a jarring hit? Or at least to be able to accompany your friends to the game and cheer without looking like a complete nincompoop? Just study this handy football primer and you'll fit right in.

Quick and Easy College Football-Watching Primer:

Tips to make you look like you belong at the game:

- Home run = baseball
  Touchdown = football
- Know what color uniforms your team is wearing, and for which end zone (the brightly colored ZONE at the END of the field) they are heading.
- Mask any extreme fondness you have for the half-time show.
- Never try to single-handedly start "the wave."
- School spirit is nice, but please limit your paraphernalia to one or two items per game. Leave the foam "#1" finger at home.
- Avoid discussing how your time could be better spent studying.
- Wait a split second before cheering to make certain you're not applauding an opposing interception.
- Never use ordinal numbers when referring to the playing field. Players do not get tackled on the "10th" yard line.

Advanced pointers:

- Dress in layers for football games. Layers give you more room to conceal flasks filled with liquor. Oh, and it might get cold out there, too.
- Mention that your team should throw to the tight end more.
- Always question the referee when a call goes against your team.
- Along those lines, scream "Intentional grounding!" whenever the opposing quarterback throws the ball out of bounds.
- Think of a creative way to insult the opposing coach (or your coach, if it is a bad season). If nothing else, "_____ sucks!" will suffice.
- Occasionally drop the word "gridiron" in casual conversation.
- If your school loses, sulk (at least for the walk out of the stadium).

College Basketball

Every college basketball team's season revolves around trying to make the NCAA Basketball Tournament. The "March Madness" tourney provides a chance for the whole school to rally around its team's quest for the national championship, but more importantly it provides a chance for the whole school to enter betting pools. Once the pairings are announced, just about every other college student xeroxes the pairings from a *USA Today* and starts a pool. These pools always have two things in common. First, they are usually won by someone whose basketball knowledge is limited to "it's the sport with all the tall people." And secondly, the winnings won't amount to much more than the $3 fee to enter, because it's always impossible to collect everyone's entrance fees. Ah, the world of high-stakes college gambling.

Other College Sports

Huh?

CHAPTER 18

THE GREEK SYSTEM

Love it or hate it, the Greek system is a big part of most campuses. While it is true that Greeks are coming under increasing fire for their elitism and irresponsibility, fraternities and sororities are time-honored American institutions and indeed, a valuable segment of the U.S. economy. Without them, T-shirt, favor, and letter-embroidering companies would go out of business quicker than you can say "Teke," not to mention the damage that would be done to the already ailing liquor industry. And where would the average American's knowledge of the Greek alphabet be if fraternities and sororities did not exist?

Fraternities

Joining a Fraternity

When shopping at different fraternities to pledge, make sure the batteries are charged in your bullshit-meter. This applies first in talking about yourself, when you say things like "I was an All-Conference linebacker . . . well, yeah, our whole team was kind of small. But we had heart . . . No, it was a private boarding school—I'm sure you've never heard of it."

Of course, it isn't just you, the rushee, who will be doing the bullshitting. Guys tend to overstate the virtues of their house when talking to rushees. Witness this real-life dialogue: "Yeah, all our pledges sleep in one big open-air dorm . . . basically just so they can get to know each other better, it's a great time . . . I had the semester of my life when I was a pledge, living up there with a great bunch of guys . . . got some of the best sleep of my life that semester." Sleeping with twenty other guys on old bunk beds in a big, chilly room has never sounded so enjoyable.

Always remember that no matter how much of a dork you may think you are, there is a fraternity on campus that is even dorkier. Every school has a few "time warp" frats; houses whose furnishings and members look like they came right out of the early '70s. Ironically enough, the people in these houses don't even do drugs.

Fraternity Myths

All fraternities take themselves too seriously. This is part of the reason why they seem so intimidating (or so laughable) to those outside them. A few fraternity myths worth clearing up:

Frat guys get laid all the time
It may seem this way to the outsider, but in fact it is often actually tougher for guys in houses to get laid. This is because most of the girls they meet are in sororities, and since sorority girls travel in packs, it is extremely hard for guys to get them alone. Which also explains why

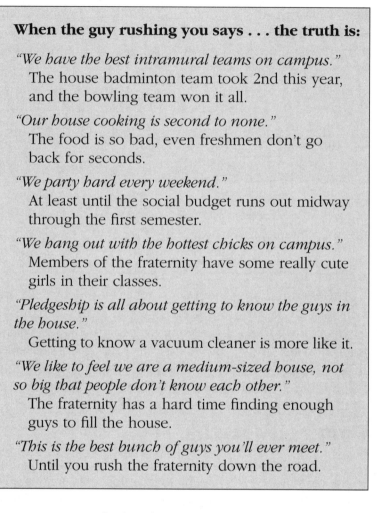

When the guy rushing you says . . . the truth is:

"We have the best intramural teams on campus."
The house badminton team took 2nd this year,
and the bowling team won it all.

"Our house cooking is second to none."
The food is so bad, even freshmen don't go
back for seconds.

"We party hard every weekend."
At least until the social budget runs out midway
through the first semester.

"We hang out with the hottest chicks on campus."
Members of the fraternity have some really cute
girls in their classes.

*"Pledgeship is all about getting to know the guys in
the house."*
Getting to know a vacuum cleaner is more like it.

*"We like to feel we are a medium-sized house, not
so big that people don't know each other."*
The fraternity has a hard time finding enough
guys to fill the house.

"This is the best bunch of guys you'll ever meet."
Until you rush the fraternity down the road.

most sorority girls decide it's time for a serious boyfriend
soon after joining a house.

Fraternity life is like the movie Animal House
Only in the sense that houses still get a kick out of
cranking Otis Day and the Knights at their parties. Frat
life gets tamer and tamer every year. Insurance liabili-
ties, increased pressure for social responsibility, and

crackdowns on drinking and pledge hazing[13] are lead-
ing to a kinder, gentler fraternal order.

All members of a given fraternity are "brothers"
While most guys do hang pretty close to the members of
their house, every house has at least one or two outcasts
the rest of the members despise and wish had never
pledged. Beware of these fraternal pariahs—they are invariably the most visible members of a house while at
the same time the house's most embarrassing represen-
tatives, and should be shunned at every opportunity.

Fraternity life is an idyllic, hassle-free existence
Most fraternities have an unofficial creed, "Any member's
personal property belongs to all brothers." So just because you bought that new Soundgarden disc don't think
that you automatically own it and can take it with you
when you graduate. Sure it's possible, but it's far more
likely that the disc will find its way into that mysterious
Black Hole of Fraternal Possessions. At least fraternity
life allows those labels Mom insisted on sewing into your
clothing to serve some purpose.

Sororities

Joining a Sorority
If your idea of a perfect college experience is to move
into a big house with a quaint Victorian downstairs waiting area, live with 20 to 80 women who are even more
neurotic than yourself, endure restrictions on drinking
and men sleeping over, put up with a nanny-like "house

---

[13] **Hazing** (*v*) - When older, established members of an organization force
younger, newer members to do humorous, degrading, or just plain stupid
things. This ritual is justified by the group-think rule of "we had to go
through it so the new guys should too".

mom," participate in misty-eyed ceremonies of sisterhood and pay more mandatory fees than you could ever imagine, then join a sorority and move in right away.

The key to sorority membership is to get the most out of your house without becoming too involved. This is especially true in big schools, whose sororities often have 150–200 members. Find a clique of good friends in the house, go to all the parties, use the house computer to type your papers, meet lots of guys, and if at all possible, avoid having to move in. Sororities at smaller schools are generally smaller and closer-knit, which means it takes even less time for the whole house to know exactly who you were with last night.

Sorority rush is a can't-miss college experience. For the women in houses, it involves two full weeks of dressing up (usually in late-summer heat), singing inspirational sorority songs over and over, and honing already-strong talents of superficial conversation.

Then comes sorority "hash", where the sorority women discuss the rushees. This gives each member a chance to cut down any rushees who aren't good enough for the house or who made her feel insecure. If a member likes a rushee that the rest of the sorority finds tacky, she will use classic clichés such as "she's a diamond in the rough," to convince her sisters to pledge the girl. In a particularly McCarthyesque tradition, some sororities don't even allow members to discuss reasons why a particular person isn't good enough for their house. All one sorority sister has to say is "I just don't think _____ is an Omega Mu," and the rushee will be turned down.

Women going through sorority rush not only get to dress up, they get to go to every house, listen to each one sing its own uniquely enlightening song, and try to appear wholesome and enthusiastic throughout. A few days later the rushees experience the "character building" of finding out which houses liked them and which houses felt the rushee wouldn't fit "in the direction we feel we're going." There is no better preparation for the deluge of job rejections senior year and beyond than rushing the Greek system.

If, after going through rush, you feel that sorority life is not for you, don't fret—you can still get into all the fraternity parties, which you will probably consider uncool and immature by the time you are an upperclassman anyway. And you will be spared the agonizing decision of which piece of sorority clothing to wear each day.

Greek Life

The Greek system certainly isn't for everyone, and in fact is loathed and reviled by many students. But massive brainwashing notwithstanding, there are some concrete reasons why so many people choose to go Greek. While it may come as a surprise that all Greek houses are different, some aspects of Greek life are similar no matter what house you join:

Instant Friends

The very act of joining a fraternity or sorority guarantees that you will make (or buy) many new friends. Sure, this fact embodies the fakeness of the whole system, but try telling that to the average freshman stuck in the dorm on Friday night with a bunch of computer science majors who would rather tap into a government defense network than a keg of beer.

Big Parties

Joining a Greek house ensures a cluttered social calendar. Most fraternities throw a party at least every other week, which means that if guys have friends in other

The *Gilligan's Island* theme party consists of renting a boat, getting lost in a storm, and ending up on a desert island. If attending, don't plan on going to your Monday classes.

houses they can drink somewhere for free almost every night, and women always have a plethora of social events to choose from. Fraternities never turn women away at parties, and females are in fact shamelessly recruited.

Sororities and fraternities hold formals, where everyone dresses up and goes to some hotel away from campus to act even stupider than usual. At a formal, pace yourself. You don't want to get completely wasted in your room even before the actual party, miss out on the open bar at the formal, and most likely pass out by 11 P.M.

Greek houses rent out local barns for quaint barn dances, where everyone dresses up like a hick, sits in the hay of some freezing barn, and attempts to square dance. Barn dances are secretly underwritten by manufacturers of bandannas, flannel shirts and "botas,"[14] not to mention the farmer who rents out his place and laughs all the way to the bank.

There are exchanges, mixers, and other such parties, where the members of an individual fraternity mingle with the members of an individual sorority. Traditionally, these parties are conceived around some ridiculous contrived Greek-letter theme such as "Escape From Alphatraz", "20,000 Phis Under The Sea", or "Delta Cong Vietnam Blow-Out."

Wardrobe Expansion

To add a new dimension to your wardrobe join a fraternity, or, even better, a sorority. Almost immediately you will receive or purchase many "Greek letter" pieces of apparel, ranging from the ubiquitous sweatshirt to tank tops, hats, shorts, sweats, and even socks. As these are all quite expensive, take note that when you buy Greek-letter clothing you are charged per letter. In other words, a Kappa Alpha Theta will spend proportionally 50 percent more money on embroidered lettering than, say, a Delta Gamma. Multiply this by, say, fifteen pieces of sorority clothing in an average sorority girl's wardrobe, and you're looking at a decent chunk of cabbage. While this may seem like a trivial point, every little difference counts when making the agonizing choice between Greek houses.

---

[14] **Botas** (*n*) - "Wine skins" that hold liquor and can be carried over one's shoulder, botas are extremely popular on cold Midwestern campuses and ski trips. They do have a fatal flaw, though—after only a few uses they take on a leathery flavor that makes you feel like you're drinking a cheap wallet.

Pre-Marriage Security

Being a Greek puts you in the unique position of being able to put an official label on a relationship. You can bind the ties with your boyfriend/girlfriend by getting lavaliered. No, this has nothing to do with that weird lamp your parents have from the '60s. Lavaliering is when a guy gives a girl a necklace with his fraternity letters. Don't fret, gentlemen, lavalieres only cost about twenty bucks. Buy a girl any other piece of jewelry that cheap and she'll throw a fit, but give her your letters and she'll get all misty-eyed. To be lavaliered means you have symbolically bonded with your lover in a joining of your Greek houses. It is exactly as cheesy as it sounds.

If you get real serious after the lavaliering, you can get pinned. This is a step before engagement and should not be taken lightly. TRANSLATION: It's OK to cheat on your boyfriend/girlfriend when lavaliered, but you'd better think twice if pinned.

Choral Practice

Fraternities and sororities love to get together and serenade each other. Any excuse (a party coming up, new pledges to haze/show off, donuts left over from breakfast to give away, et cetera) will do for a serenade. When a house comes over to serenade, everyone in the house being serenaded is supposed to gather on the stairs or the porch to listen. The number of people who gather to listen to the serenade is good judge of the social standing of any particular house. For example, if a "good" sorority is being serenaded by a "so-so" fraternity only about half the sorority members will gather for the serenade, but if a "hot" fraternity comes calling, the sisters will fight for position at the front.

How to Have a Greek Relationship in 10 Easy Steps

1. Notice cute guy/girl.

2. Make sure he/she's in the right house (you must be both personality-compatible and house-compatible).

3. Have friend introduce you, make conversation for 5–20 minutes.

4. Ignore person for next 3 weeks.

5. Have friend set you up for dance. "Mash" at dance. Go home alone.

6. If you talk the next day, you're dating.

7. Exchange Greek clothing. Spend lots of time together. Ignore friends who aren't dating people in same house. Sleep over at each other's rooms.

8. Get "lavaliered." Allocate drawer in room for lover.

9. Get in fights. Look for sympathy in each other's friends. Get really drunk. End relationship.

10. Scam on friends of ex-girl/boyfriend.

Greek Week

Most schools with a large Greek population have a big, self-congratulatory "Greek Week" full of parties, games, and publicity-generating "community service" (the real reason fraternities and sororities exist—or didn't someone tell you?). The best thing you can do during Greek Week is to be entrepreneurial and get a piece of the action on the official Greek Week shirts. Since every Greek on campus is supposed to wear one to kick off the week, whoever sells the shirts is sure to make a bundle. Greek Week is also a great time to pad your résumé by getting on a committee of some sort (Greeks love committees). Maybe next year you can be chairperson!

The Greek Cycle

Phase One

Rush houses, let houses lavish you with sales pitches, parties, etc. Join a house, marvel at how cool everyone is, superficially meet new friends. At parties look around in wide-eyed wonder at all the beautiful people.

Phase Two

Go through pledgeship. Become thoroughly brainwashed by "best house on campus." Experience annoying drudgework and/or hazing "to help you get to know your fellow pledges." At parties pour beer for hours on end.

Phase Three

Wear Greek letters constantly and proudly. Involve yourself in numerous house activities. Spend every minute at house, develop many close friendships. Overzealously put new pledges to work. At parties drink heavily and stay up till 4 a.m.

Phase Four

Hold major office in house. Enjoy elite decision-making privileges. Organize efforts "for the good of the house." Feel the satisfaction of doing something important. At parties socialize with your hundreds of friends on campus.

Phase Five

Become increasingly sick of house environment. Find younger members looking up to you, but don't really have time or inclination to get to know them. Feel vague dissatisfaction with whole Greek system. At parties, talk with older friends about how much more fun everything used to be.

Phase Six

Isolate yourself completely from house. Everyone seems so young and immature these days! Bitterly slam your house and the Greek system as a whole to others. Stop going to house parties.

CHAPTER 19

ROAD TRIPS

Road trips are an integral part of the college experience. Every month or so, when one's underwear starts feeling too tight and that vague unease starts to build, it is time to hit the road, Jack, saddle up a posse, and get outta town. Note that going home for the weekend is a cop-out and does not qualify as a road trip. Unless, of course, your parents are out of town and you bring a bunch of friends home with you, which makes for one of the coolest road trips of all. At least until you have to clean up your house on Sunday morning with a bunch of hungover friends demanding breakfast . . . but why dwell on the negatives?

Road Trip Tips

- A car is usually a good start. If *you* own a car, however, use any excuse not to take it, as nothing puts more wear-and-tear on your auto than a road trip.

- The car you end up taking will inevitably be one of those "college" cars, usually a hand-me-down that has been in someone's family for a decade or so. Meaning the auto will run, sure, but any number of minor things will not work (such as windows, door locks, turn signals, windshield wipers, and, worst of all, the stereo). Still, these features give the car personality, especially if it's a funny old car to begin with (like a Pinto or Gremlin). A good college car will take on a near-mythical status among your social circle.

- A car can get gross pretty quickly on road trips. Note: nothing is harder to clean than Cheetos residue.

Use any excuse not to use your auto for a road trip. Nothing puts more wear and tear on a car.

- Always leave on Thursday. Attending your Friday classes before a road trip isn't even an option.

- Be extremely leery of road trips with members of the opposite sex. The ensuing scumminess, inevitable arguments, and wrong turns are experiences best not shared with your current flame. Unless, that is, you want to see your boyfriend/girlfriend at his or her most vulnerable, in which case catch them waking up with stale Dr. Pepper and Pringles breath after a nap in a hot car.

- While you don't want to actually *hit the road* with a girlfriend/boyfriend, visiting one is an obvious reason for a road trip. You don't have to be in a serious relationship to visit someone, either. An old high school flame, your winter/summer vacation scam, a friend's cute sibling; any vague love or lust is a good excuse for this particular type of road trip, which is known as a Nookie Run.

- Spontaneity is a key road trip element. Anything can be an excuse for a spontaneous road trip. Some proven winners:
  - Any other campus
  - White Castle
  - Graceland
  - A Phish concert
  - Florida
  - Large bodies of water
  - The Fishing Hall of Fame in Hayward, Wisconsin (look for the giant walleye)

- The 24-Hour L.L. Bean flagship store in Freeport, Maine

- "It's snowing in them hills." Need more be said?

- Getting to your destination is usually more fun than being there. Once you get there, chances are pretty good that you'll spend most of your time in some bar hanging out with the people you made the trip with, talking about everyone back at school and occasionally striking out in a pathetic manner with a member of the opposite sex.

- The ride back sucks. It always does. Don't count on conversation to make it go by quickly, as hangovers, and lack of sleep will make the minutes pass like hours.

- The license plate game you used to play in the car with your parents may not cut it, but amusing mental games can help pass the time, especially on long trips. Try Brady Bunch trivia, "Name That Tune" on the local Muzak station, or Road Bingo (using squares like "dead animal", "abandoned Stuckeys", or "suction-cup Garfield on a left rear window"). If games like these are too intellectual, you can always make fun of passing motorists, like the way you used to write "HELP—I'M BEING KIDNAPPED" on a fogged-up window of your school bus in grade school.

- Something will always go wrong on a road trip. Feel lucky if you just get off at a wrong exit. Join an automobile club such as AAA beforehand, or at least travel with a member, as AAA members get free towing, jump starts, and lots of neat maps.

Road Munchies

- A gas credit card can go a long way. Especially if it doesn't belong to you. Essential foodstuffs such as Combos, Slushees, and microwave burritos can be charged up, as well as trashy magazines, road maps, lottery tickets, cheap shades, and other niceties.

- Known laws of nutrition are suspended as long as you are in a car. The greasier and more preservative-laden the food, the better. When in doubt, grab anything with a factory-stamped price on the package, i.e. any products by Frito-Lay, Hostess, or their unsung, incredibly cheap rival, Little Debbie.

- Caffeine, caffeine, caffeine. Coffee, iced tea, and best of all, Diet Mountain Dew.

ROAD FOOD CHART	
Bad	**Good**
Corn-on-the cob	Corn dog
Pork chops	Pork rinds
Beef Wellington	Beef jerky
Milk	Milk of magnesia
Fondue	Mountain Dew
French onion soup	French fries
Toast	Tostitos
Flaming Saginaki cheese	Cheetos
Chocolate mousse	Chocolate milkshake
Chicken cacciatore	Chicken McNuggets

Spring Break

The most important road trip of the year is, of course, Spring Break. A detailed primer on Spring Break behavior would be banal—if you feel you need this, any number of low-budget, mid-Eighties movies will do for reference.

Studying Abroad

The ultimate road trip is to study abroad for a semester. If by junior year the college routine is becoming a wee bit mundane, you may want to look into this. Most colleges have their own study abroad programs at different foreign locales. And even if your particular school's program happens to be in Beirut, the study abroad office will offer a wide variety of programs through other colleges in different places. You should be able to find a school to your liking in any country you wish.

Yeah, but doesn't it cost a lot to study abroad?

Cost, schmost. These programs are surprisingly competitive with the cost of a regular semester at school. Plus how can you put a price on the experience? (Or so you tell your parents).

OK, but what if I don't know the language?

Fake it. (Just kidding.) Again, the language barrier is no problem. Your classes (unless noted otherwise) will be in English with American instructors and other American students. If the language thing really worries you, you can always study in England.

But won't I miss my friends?

Au contraire. You'll become a Euro-snob. You'll laugh at the trite things you used to do at school. You'll become pale, slim, and will develop an unhealthy tint to your skin. You'll smoke unfiltered cigarettes and drink herbal tea. Upon returning to the States your "friends" will seem immature and less worldly. You'll pepper your speech with little foreign phrases you picked up. You will spend Friday nights alone in your room reading Nietzsche. The effects of this will last until you sit down in front of the TV one day to watch some public broadcasting and mistakenly turn on *Friends.* The mere sight of Joey and Chandler is enough to jar even the most bohemian Euro-snobs back to their senses, and back to the wonderful embraces of Americana.

So going to Europe is going to turn me into a pompous jerk?

You'll get over it. Besides, studying abroad may even help you appreciate the good ol' U.S. of A.

I hear I won't be able to plug my hair dryer into European outlets.

Buy an adapter, you twit.

I'm convinced. Where do I sign up?

Once again, just go to your school's study abroad office. You'll be glad you did.

CHAPTER 20

GRADUATION AND THE GREAT VOID BEYOND

Editors' Note:
This chapter should definitely **not** be read until you have been in college for a year or two. Put this book on the shelf for a while, and wait until you're a junior or senior to read this part. The jaded, harsh opinions and realities contained in the next few pages could send any cheerful high school senior into a downward spiral of pointless, bitter cynicism.

THE REAL WORLD: AN ANALYSIS

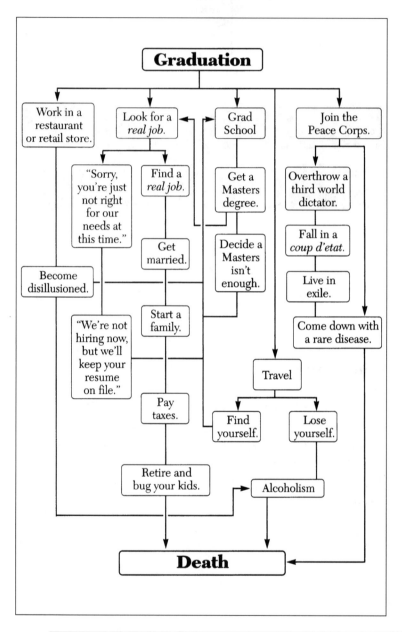

The Job Search

Much of your senior year (and/or the year or years after graduation) will consist of trying to find a job. The job search is a scary taste of the real world. All of a sudden, words like résumé, cover letter, interview, plant trip, networking, suit, and ulcer become part of your everyday vocabulary.

Résumés

A résumé is a one-page summary of your life's achievements. No, this doesn't mean achievements like the number of people you have slept with, or the fact that you once put away nine shots of tequila without puking. A résumé should highlight things that will impress a future employer, not a crowded bar.

The key to a good résumé is creativity. This can be done even if you've done nothing but sleep twelve hours a day, get C's, and rent *Caddyshack* seven times a semester. The résumé on the following page shows how even the most marginal college career can be made to look impressive.

Internships

An internship is a situation in which, either while in school or directly out of it, you work for a company for a short period of time (such as a summer break) to "learn the ropes" of whatever it is you want to do. Sort of like being the Sorcerer's Apprentice, except that good sorcerers are tough to find these days. Internships can be part-time or full-time, and you can often obtain course credit for them. Internships can be a great experience, but have one drawback—most of them don't pay. Still, even though you're working for free, internships can get your foot in the door, which is especially important if

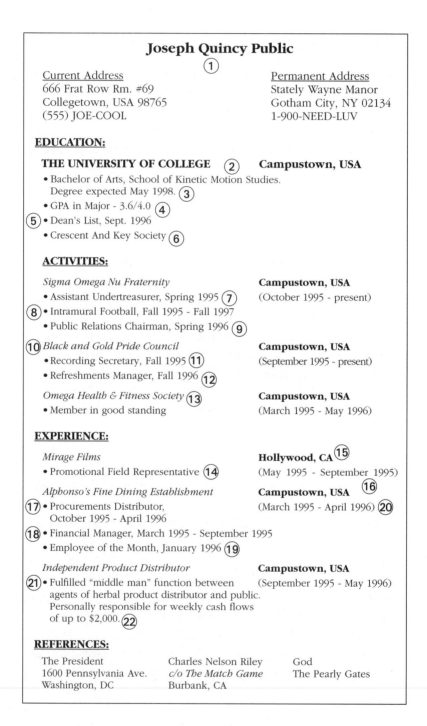

Joseph Quincy Public ①

Current Address
666 Frat Row Rm. #69
Collegetown, USA 98765
(555) JOE-COOL

Permanent Address
Stately Wayne Manor
Gotham City, NY 02134
1-900-NEED-LUV

EDUCATION:

THE UNIVERSITY OF COLLEGE ②　　**Campustown, USA**
- Bachelor of Arts, School of Kinetic Motion Studies.
  Degree expected May 1998. ③
- GPA in Major - 3.6/4.0 ④
⑤ • Dean's List, Sept. 1996
- Crescent And Key Society ⑥

ACTIVITIES:

Sigma Omega Nu Fraternity　　　　　　**Campustown, USA**
- Assistant Undertreasurer, Spring 1995 ⑦　(October 1995 - present)
⑧ • Intramural Football, Fall 1995 - Fall 1997
- Public Relations Chairman, Spring 1996 ⑨

⑩ *Black and Gold Pride Council*　　　　**Campustown, USA**
- Recording Secretary, Fall 1995 ⑪　　(September 1995 - present)
- Refreshments Manager, Fall 1996 ⑫

Omega Health & Fitness Society ⑬　　**Campustown, USA**
- Member in good standing　　　　　　(March 1995 - May 1996)

EXPERIENCE:

Mirage Films　　　　　　　　　　**Hollywood, CA** ⑮
- Promotional Field Representative ⑭　(May 1995 - September 1995)

Alphonso's Fine Dining Establishment　**Campustown, USA** ⑯
⑰ • Procurements Distributor,　　　　(March 1995 - April 1996) ⑳
  October 1995 - April 1996
⑱ • Financial Manager, March 1995 - September 1995
- Employee of the Month, January 1996 ⑲

Independent Product Distributor　　　**Campustown, USA**
㉑ • Fulfilled "middle man" function between　(September 1995 - May 1996)
  agents of herbal product distributor and public.
  Personally responsible for weekly cash flows
  of up to $2,000. ㉒

REFERENCES:

The President
1600 Pennsylvania Ave.
Washington, DC

Charles Nelson Riley
c/o The Match Game
Burbank, CA

God
The Pearly Gates

Reading Between The Lines of A Good Résumé *(left)*

1. Using your middle initial makes you look more important.
2. In other words, a Physical Education major.
3. or 1999 or 2000 . . .
4. Well, at least the classes *you* considered "major" . . . who's counting anyway?
5. Your name actually in your friend Dean's phone list since 1995, but you're being modest.
6. Got your keys out of a locked car with a crescent wrench once.
7. Ran house NCAA basketball tourney pool.
8. Well, at least you signed up for the teams.
9. Told girls in Psychology 172 class about big party.
10. Went to football games wearing school colors.
11. Taped "away" games on VCR.
12. Brought friends hot dogs and Cokes during halftime.
13. Weightlifted sporadically in fraternity weight room. Got bench press up to 205 lbs.!
14. Dressed up as Barney for kid's parties.
15. Well, they shot the TV show it was based on in Hollywood.
16. Actually quit after five days but school didn't start until September.
17. Put french fries in deep fryer, retrieved them 90 seconds later, and applied salt.
18. Promoted to night cash register guy.
19. Boss gave you pat on the back one afternoon.
20. Fired for giving free pizza puffs to buddies.
21. Sold dope to dorm residents.
22. It was an especially good week.

you're looking for a career in entertainment, communications, or other fields that are tough to break into. Just be very clear as to what you are going to gain from a particular internship, as few things are more frustrating than stuffing envelopes all summer for free for someone who doesn't teach you anything or help you make any connections.

Networking

No, this does not refer to the crisis that arises when the cable TV goes out. Networking is the all-too "real world" way of finding jobs, where getting a job is based more on *who* you know than *what* you know. It's almost like self-advertising; tell literally everyone you talk to that you are looking for a particular job, and sooner or later someone will know someone who has a cousin who is, say, a bigwig at the Utility Muffin Research Kitchen. This applies to your parents and their friends, too. *Especially* to your parents and their friends—in today's job market there is no shame in nepotism.

Interviewing

Many students, particularly those in marketable majors like business or engineering, find they spend more time their senior year interviewing than studying. Placement services on campus allow the tiresome job-search process to be done with university resources, and should be taken advantage of if you are set on finding a corporate job right out of college. With that said, however, it must be noted that there are a zillion more fun things to do with your senior year (most involving heavy drinking), and the stress of senior year interviewing may best be put off until graduation, when you can live at home and take your frustrations out on your parents.

If companies are interviewing on your campus (meaning *they* are coming to *you*), simply submit your résumé to your college's placement office and let them know which companies you are interested in. The placement office will soon inform you which of these companies considered you worthy of 15 minutes of their time, and will assign you an interview. If *no one* even grants you an interview, it may be time to take a closer look at your résumé. Does your résumé state your (fully embellished) qualifications? Did you spell-check it? For that matter, did you even *type* it?

If companies that you are interested in aren't interviewing on your campus, you will have to search them out, call them up, and mail or fax them your résumé. When you mail out résumés, companies will either contact you to set up an interview or they'll send you a *bong letter.* A bong letter tells you in a polite, businesslike manner that you are underqualified for the job. Contrary to popular belief, bong letters were *not* named for the device which potheads inevitably fire up when they receive one of these in the mail. No, this "bong" is the sound of the gong of rejection (does anyone still remember Chuck Barris and J.P. Morgan?) Bong letters traditionally must be posted on your bulletin board or refrigerator to serve as daily reminders of what a loser you are.

Once you have secured an interview it's time to research exactly what it is the company does. It's not as easy as it sounds. The only information your placement office usually gives you is the corporation's annual report. Annual reports traditionally consist of mindless gibberish and financial data manipulated so shareholders have no idea how close the company is to Chapter 11. Still, you need to obtain some sort of information on your prospective employer, so do some research. Job chances go downhill pretty quickly when you tell an interviewer you've heard his fiber optics corporation makes really good pet foods.

Interviewing is one of the few times in college when your personal appearance must be at its best. Wear deodorant, avoid garlicky foods, and leave your baseball hat and backpack home. Women dressing for an interview should strive for a plain yet competent look; wear something resembling men's clothing and forget the big hair. Men should wear a dark, conservative suit with the proper accessories (in other words, white socks are out and avoid fish ties).

The key to the interview itself is to stand out, but in a pleasant, non-threatening sort of way. Never appear *too* different or blessed with *too* much personality. Corporations are large, homogeneous bodies, and corporate employees are intimidated by anyone who appears remotely "offbeat". Many employees who conduct interviews are low-level nobodies (important executives have neither the time nor the desire to deal with entry-level hiring), and if you come across as an eccentric go-getter to these types they will find you threatening to their positions.

Every interviewer will be different. Some will spend most of the time telling *you* all about their company, while others will give you a barrage of irritating, insipid questions like "Where do you see yourself in five years?" "If you could invite one famous person to dinner, who would it be?" or "Who led the AL in RBIs in 1974?" (Jeff Burroughs of the Texas Rangers, by the way). The best thing to do is keep your composure and, above all, *tell interviewers whatever they want to hear.* In other words, lie.

Results

There is a good chance that even if you spend your entire senior year kissing up to half the Fortune 500, you still won't have a job on graduation day. This may actually be a blessing; you now have the opportunity to relax, travel, and do all those things you wanted to while you're still young and independent. Of course, you will have to live at home and do manual labor or work in a restaurant or retail store to pay for all this.

For those of you who do get a job out of school; congratulations—you have just entered the Rat Race. Time to put on a suit every morning, put in 60-hour work weeks, kiss the ass of your superior, and become a full-fledged *grown-up* in no time. In the beginning you will probably envy your jobless friends who are going out every night or backpacking around the globe. But after corporate philosophy has been drummed into you for a year or so you any second thoughts will disappear. Your slacker friends just don't have their priorities straight like you do.

Grad School

Until recently, there was a myth that you went to college for four years, graduated, got a decent job, and settled down to become a productive cog in society's wheels. Today this interpretation is about as valid as the geocentric universe theory.

It is still possible to graduate in four years and get a job, but most likely you'll find yourself adrift in a sea of uncertainty after the umbilical cord of college is cut. Don't fret, though—this is America, land of opportunity, and there is a way to continue the fairy tale existence of college: *graduate school.*

Granted, some students know from the outset that grad school looms on their horizon. Future doctors, psychiatrists, and lawyers have a good excuse to pursue further education—it's required. But many people go on to grad school for lack of anything better to do. What of the lost soul who is selling cars with a Bachelors in English and a Masters in Sociology? Why does college turn out so many of these aimless academic wasteoids?

Still, for more and more undergraduates, grad school is the answer. Law school admissions in particular have swelled, partly because everyone who ever watched *Law and Order* thinks "Wouldn't it be great to dress that nicely and work with beautiful people all day? I could do that." Ask typical students entering law school if they feel a calling to uphold justice or if the prospect of a six-figure salary and a BMW convertible appeals to them—the latter would certainly be the more honest answer. An even more honest answer, however, is "What else can I do with my History, Political Science, or American Studies degree?"

Yeah, grad school is a pretty smart way to avoid making any tough decisions. You get to stay in your little plastic bubble for a few more years. But it's not as easy as it seems—this extended vacation from reality has its costs:

Money. Graduate educations are not cheap. If you want an inexpensive one, watch syndicated TV reruns—schools abound for truck driving, cosmetics, and whatever Sally Struthers is currently pitching. A grad school worth attending will cost you dearly, meaning you must either grapple with financial aid and government grants or convince your parents that your undergraduate degree isn't worth spit. Either way, though it may be impossible to picture, you will have even less spending money than you did as an undergrad.

Workload. Much like the upper levels of Super Mario Brothers, some graduate school programs can be a real bitch. Mickey Mouse classes are a thing of the past as you work to dissect cadavers, make law review, and transcribe ancient tomes into Esperanto.

Social Life. As a grad student you become a social outcast on campus. Many of your peers are in their thirties and forties, and even the straight-out-of-college grad student feels too old and mature to relate to the average undergrad. Due to your monk-like study habits and general lack of friends, your social skills will regress to the level of a young child raised in the wilderness. Watch yourself closely or you may also fall victim to the grad student "look": stubble, matted hair, corduroys, an antiquated bicycle and a dilapidated backpack.

Graduation

Good luck. You'll need it.

Genuflect at the alma mater statue for good luck.

APPENDIX

THINGS WE MAY HAVE MISSED

Ten things to know before entering college:

1. Your school's name
2. How to pronounce "Camus"
3. Your tolerance
4. Wash white clothes separately
5. The shelf life of cold pizza
6. The shelf life of warm beer
7. When you're stuck, answer "B"
8. Time and channel *Politically Incorrect* comes on
9. Madonna is not considered "college music"
10. The difference between *latté* and *au lait*

Ten things you are likely to lose at college:

1. Your morals
2. A taste for veal
3. The belief that a college education can actually get you a good job
4. An unblemished credit rating
5. Your fake ID
6. About 1500 hours of sleep
7. All those Cross pens you got for high school graduation
8. Assuming you had it to begin with, your virginity
9. Your cookies on a number of occasions
10. Your high school friends

Ten things you stand to gain at college:

1. 10 to 20 pounds
2. Mounting debt
3. A taste for coffee
4. Political correctness
5. Self-sufficiency
6. Multiple sweatshirts
7. Proficiency in the deft art of brownnosing
8. A taste for malted beverages
9. Lifelong friends
10. A clue

Ten key words for classes you should avoid:

1. *Micro* anything
2. *Macro* anything
3. *Bio* anything
4. *Neuro* anything
5. *Advanced* anything *Theory*
6. *Quantum* anything

Ten key words for classes you should avoid: (cont.)

7. *History* of anything
8. *Geomorphology* of anything
9. *Socio* anything
10. *Symbolism in Ancient Chinese* anything

Ten key words for classes you should take:

1. Anything *101*
2. Anything *Kinesiology*
3. Anything *Communications*
4. *Home* anything
5. Anything for *Beginners*
6. Anything *Observation*
7. Anything *Study Skills*
8. *Fashion* anything
9. Anything *Weaving*
10. *Films of the Eighties*

Ten reasons to skip class class:

1. It's not like they're going to cancel it
2. You can't find a pen
3. What? And miss *Days of Our Lives?*
4. So you can be first in line at the cafeteria for green bean casserole
5. You wanted to wait for the mailman to give you the new Columbia Music House catelogs
6. You *paid* for the snooze button—use it!
7. You need to rest up for a big night out
8. Those guys in *Animal House* never went to class, and they turned out OK
9. Bad case of writer's cramp
10. Because you can

Ten reasons to go to class:

1. That special someone
2. It's Monday—all the Putt-Putt courses are closed
3. Neglectful roommate forgot to pay your heating bill
4. Neglectful roommate forgot to pay your cable bill
5. The comforting drone of the instructor and the relaxing scrape of chalk
6. They're showing a cool movie
7. Everybody else is
8. Sore wrist keeps you out of the bowling alley
9. They'd never think to look for you there
10. Final exam

Ten things to do in your fifth year of college:

1. Talk about the "good ol' days"
2. Change your major
3. Finally memorize the school fight song
4. Find out the plural of syllabus
5. Try once again to sell back those obscure poli-sci books
6. Sit at home on Fridays while the youngsters rabble-rouse
7. Learn how to fill out unemployment forms
8. Start a vegetable garden
9. Count on one hand the friends you have left
10. Graduate

Biography

Clark Benson and Alex Gordon have known each other since the 2nd grade, when they shared a cubby tray in Mrs. Pringle's class.

Clark attended the University of Illinois at Champaign-Urbana where he wrote features for the *Daily Illini* and even penned the infamous "Campus Scout" column in the grand tradition of Gene Shalit and Artie Johnson.

Alex attended the University of Michigan where he worked as an editor for the *Michigan Daily* and created the weekly "Alex About Town" column. Alex also has a graduate degree in journalism from the Medill School of Journalism at Northwestern University.

In addition to their writing experience, both Clark and Alex were well-rounded college animals. Clark majored in finance and was a member of a concert production group, worked for the campus radio station, managed and tended bar at a campus nightclub, was an officer of his fraternity, and ate his fair share of late night burritos.

Alex majored in his native tongue, English, and was president of his dorm floor, played two years of lacrosse, wrote comedy sketches for a university improv group, worked at a sandwich joint and as a sorority busboy (only because of the free Pop-Tarts).

Clark currently resides in Los Angeles and is the founder of the OASIS CD Listening Station Program, a music marketing company, as well as a partner in the Off/Beat Music record store in Redondo Beach, CA.

Alex lives in Chicago where he is the managing editor of Ziff-Davis *Internet Underground Magazine* and still holds out hope that some day he'll take over the "Goofus and Gallant" column in *Highlights for Kids*.

Clark and Alex both miss dearly the $2 pitcher nights.